The PEDAGOGY of CONFIDENCE

Inspiring High Intellectual Performance in Urban Schools

The PEDAGOGY of CONFIDENCE

Inspiring High Intellectual Performance in Urban Schools

YVETTE JACKSON

Foreword by
Reuven Feuerstein

TEACHERS COLLEGE PRESS

TEACHERS COLLEGE | COLUMBIA UNIVERSITY

NEW YORK AND LONDON

This book is dedicated to the memory of

Asa Hilliard III
(Nana Baffour Amankwatia, II)

whose teachings have emboldened so many to recognize
their African heritage for the gift it is

Pedagogy of Confidence is a registered trademark

Published by Teachers College Press, 1234 Amsterdam Avenue, New York, NY 10027

Copyright © 2011 by Teachers College, Columbia University

Library of Congress Cataloging-in-Publication Data

Jackson, Yvette.
    The pedagogy of confidence : inspiring high intellectual performance in urban schools /
Yvette Jackson ; foreword by Reuven Feuerstein.
    p.   cm.
Includes bibliographical references and index.
ISBN 978-0-8077-5223-4 (pbk. : alk. paper)
ISBN 978-0-8077-5224-1 (hardcover : alk. paper)
    1. Children with social disabilities—Education—United States.   2. City children—
Education—United States.   3. Achievement motivation—United States.   I. Title.

LC4091.J33 2011
371.009173'2—dc22   2010051716

ISBN 978-0-8077-5223-4 (paper)
ISBN 978-0-8077-5224-1 (hardcover)

Printed on acid-free paper
Manufactured in the United States of America

18 17 16 15   8 7 6 5

Contents

PART III   The Structures

Foreword

THIS BOOK BY DR. YVETTE JACKSON is a tour de force that brings the reader into a tapestry rich in colors and forms reflecting the stormy feelings generated by early childhood memories of encounters with educators who openly expressed the generalized and well-accepted lack of belief in the capacities of students of color. This lack of belief was (and too often still is) reflected in the disproportionate numbers of African American and Hispanic/Latino children in special education programs, which often act as custodial care programs rather than learning environments. Nobody could deny the sad reality: The manifest level of functioning of many from these populations was indeed unacceptably low. But did this mean that their potential was as low as the functioning they demonstrated in conventional intelligence test situations? In particular, was the demonstrated poverty of academic communication skills obscuring the true capacities of these children? Yvette would not accept the notion that these levels of achievement were fixed and immutable, as promulgated by ideologies of hereditarily fixed intelligence, such as those represented in Arthur Jensen's conception of the innate nature of intelligence. These ideologies propelled Yvette in her ardent search for more optimistic views about human modifiability. Her own experience had made her well aware of the discrepancy between the way she was perceived by too many and the realization that she could and did do better than those perceptions.

I cannot forget my first encounter with Yvette. She had been alerted by Professor Abraham Tannenbaum of Columbia University's Teachers College, her dissertation mentor, about a series of presentations I would be holding at the national conference of the Association for Supervision and Curriculum Development. She approached me prior to my presentations and said, "Sir, your theory and approach are what I had been looking for for so long." Prior to this first encounter, she had fervently studied both the theory of Structural Cognitive Modifiability (SCM) and its applied systems,

finding the scientific support to advance her mission to find tools that
would actually modify the structure of the learning process for those African
American students subjected to various forms of disadvantage outside and
inside of school. Her research was aimed mainly at discovering the hidden
capacities of these students and pointing out that many of those who were
considered underperforming or retarded could display gifted behaviors
when given the appropriate learning conditions.

Her persistence was by far more extreme than anything I had ever dared
to exhibit. She was driven to find evidence that low or retarded functioning
could be hiding high potential, and she was committed in her belief that
the main goal of education should be to reveal these capacities by constructing support for them. This quest was her first step in the development of the
Pedagogy of Confidence. Like the miners of the California Gold Rush, she
searched for the most efficient equipment that could bring forth the gold of
giftedness where too few had been willing to even consider its existence.

After having mastered the theory of Structural Cognitive Modifiability
and Mediated Learning Experience, she continued coursework at Teachers
College. She made a concerted effort to show the power of the Instrumental Enrichment program through her doctoral dissertation, which was entitled "The Identification of Potential Giftedness in Disadvantaged Students."
The rigorously performed research done in Atlanta, Georgia, permitted her
to employ a highly controlled and ingeniously elaborated statistical analysis to reveal the gold she had been searching for. An intensive and well-
structured educational program of Instrumental Enrichment applied over
a period of three years had in fact uncovered the deeply buried potential
of giftedness in students considered as low functioning. But she was not
content to write a dissertation and leave it to languish on a shelf. Instead,
she devoted her life to using her findings and the methodology she had
applied for identifying giftedness where it had for so long gone unrecognized. The position she assumed as Director of Gifted Programs for the
New York City Public Schools provided her with experiences that enabled
her to formulate in both conceptual and practical ways the essential conditions that would turn the low functioning of students into manifest levels
of high intellectual performance in school and achievement in life. It is
these rich, diverse, and emotionally ridden experiences that are crystallized
in the Pedagogy of Confidence.

Dr. Jackson's confrontation with resistance even by those who should
have adopted her approach has made her become more realistic about the
investment necessary to reach the desired goal of manifesting high intellectual performance in poor students from urban environments. She has learned

that it is not only the students whose learning must be modified. There are the teachers, who must become convinced that indeed the intelligence and the intellectual level of their students can be meaningfully altered. There are the parents, whose support both emotionally and behaviorally is a clear determinant of the necessary change in their children. There is the whole community, whose support is needed through advocacy and philanthropic activities. And last, but not least, there are the governmental authorities, who must become not only aware of the truth but also the ardent promoters of a system based on belief in the vast potential of disadvantaged students. It will take all of these to make the necessary investment to turn the modifiability of the potential of these students into a massive and extended phenomenon of achievement and success in society at large.

In reading this very impressive book, I feel indeed that I have found in Dr. Yvette Jackson not only an interpreter but actually a constructor of a powerful edifice. By using some of the stones of the theory of Structural Cognitive Modifiability and Mediated Learning Experience, along with the associated applied systems, she has constructed the Pedagogy of Confidence. Under this concept she certainly covers a wide array of issues related to children of groups labeled as "minorities," who must struggle to reach the higher echelons of society. Her major concern is to assist educators in creating the environmental, psychological, and educational conditions that will support and encourage the upward mobility of students who grow up in conditions of poverty and discrimination. She considers the advancement of the students and the teachers on whom they depend as possible only in a climate of confidence. The unsurpassable barriers raised by psychological and educational selective methods—such as testing the level of functioning of students rather than evaluating their modifiability via learning of cognitive processes—have left many otherwise gifted children outside of the area identified as "excellence." In this book, Dr. Jackson carefully confronts each one of these barriers and demonstrates that, given the appropriate learning conditions, students can become capable of surmounting even the highest barriers. The book presents a great wealth of pedagogical methods to instill the confidence so essential to overcoming these barriers. The in-depth elaboration of psychological, educational, and social concepts she presents supports the large and ingenious inventory of pedagogical tools she offers— tools designed to stimulate achievement and upward mobility for those students who depend on teachers to make this advancement possible.

There is no doubt that this book will make the reader aware of the existence of the great potential of underperforming students for realizing high intellectual performance. The work Dr. Yvette Jackson is doing with the

National Urban Alliance for Effective Education is certainly not only highly promising but also a very effective way to build the confidence of teachers so that they may go forward to change the destiny of masses of what can become *formerly* "disadvantaged underperforming" students.

—Professor Reuven Feuerstein
Chairman and Founder
International Center for the
Enhancement of Learning Potential
Jerusalem, Israel

Acknowledgments

FIRST AND FOREMOST I thank Reuven Feuerstein for providing the world with his transformative theory and practices, which are the foundation of the Pedagogy of Confidence. I am also humbled to be able to thank him for his personal guidance as my mentor.

The Pedagogy of Confidence has been more than thirty years in the making, and as with any odyssey of such duration, scores of people have assisted me along the way. I thank them for their support, guidance, and expertise in helping me bring this book to reality.

I return to the beginning years of the odyssey and thank administrators such as Lois Jameson, who, as the principal of the school in which I taught, allowed me to turn my beliefs into classroom practice. I am grateful also to Gladys Pack, whose coaching enabled me to lead the Title IV-C grant that began my foray as a professional developer in gifted education.

I offer special acknowledgment to Charlotte Frank, former Executive Director of Curriculum and Instruction for the New York City Public Schools, who had faith in me and elegantly mentored my development as Director of the Gifted Unit. The knowledge gained there has been expanded and deepened through my association with many esteemed educators and psychologists, such as Art Costa, Linda Darling-Hammond, Asa Hilliard III, Jabari Mahiri, Augusta Mann, Pedro Noguera, and Joseph Renzulli. I thank Askia Davis, whose reflection-provoking discussions, affirmations, and leadership during those early years were (and continue to be) catalysts for me to broaden the scope of my practice.

In the early 1990s I had the great fortune of working with David Hyerle, whose Thinking Maps® are integral tools in the High Operational Practices of the Pedagogy of Confidence. I thank him for this seminal contribution.

The National Urban Alliance for Effective Education has been my home for almost twenty years. I extend profound appreciation to its founder and president, Eric Cooper, for inviting me to be his partner, providing me the organizational base through which I could cultivate and codify the Pedagogy of Confidence. I am also grateful to my colleagues and friends at the National Urban Alliance for being muses in the crafting of the High Operational Practices of the Pedagogy of Confidence: Ahmes Askia, Ravit Bar Av, Arlene Cassello, LaVerne Flowers, Marlyn Lawrence, Alexis Leitgeb, Eyka Luby, Veronica McDermott, Mamie Merrifield, Denise Nessel, Stefanie Rome, Nicole Walters, Evangeline Wise, Marilyn Zaretsky, and all of the NUA mentors whose excellent professional development leadership has rekindled confidence in teachers throughout our partner districts. I feel equally deep gratitude for the executive team, Patricia Haith, Ken Lubetsky, and Val Zeman, whose oversight and endless assistance have enabled me to focus on the writing of this book.

I also thank the individuals who allowed me to cite their work or tell their stories in this book: Ahmes Askia, Cynthia Brictson, Askia Davis, Camile Earle-Dennis, Carlos Garcia, Shirley Graham, Jason Marwon Hannon, Donald Harper, Dan Jett, Audra Jordan, Alexis Leitgeb, Carlton Long, Jabari Mahiri, Jay Marks, Connie McNally, Denise Nessel, Mary Oberg, Barbara Pulliam-Davis, John Ramos, Francisa Sánchez, and Geoff Suddreth.

I offer many thanks as well to those who do not know me personally but have influenced my thinking: James Comer, Lisa Delpit, Carol Dweck, Geneva Gay, Eric Jensen, Gloria Ladson-Billings, Robert Sternberg, and Robert Sylwester. I pay special tribute to David Whyte, whose poetry inspired me to use a bold voice to share my beliefs.

I extend my earnest appreciation to Brian Ellerbeck, Executive Acquisition Editor at Teachers College Press, who encouraged me to write this book and had the patience to withstand the many iterations of the manuscript. I also thank Karl Nyberg and Peter Sieger at Teachers College Press for their efforts in shepherding the book through the production process and for having had the brilliance to assign Lynne Frost to be its copy editor and typesetter. Her tireless creative genius provided the magic to transform the manuscript into this final product.

Lastly, I thank my entire family—siblings, in-laws, nieces, and nephews—for their endless cheerleading. But most of all, I thank my husband, Howard Gollub, whose editorial guidance, edifying insight, love, and confidence in me created the beacon of light that has guided me throughout the twenty years of our life together.

Introduction

THE PURPOSE OF THIS BOOK is to rekindle educators' belief in the vast capacity of their urban students and to restore their confidence in their own ability to inspire high intellectual performance by these students.

I have worked with many school districts across America where underachievement has become the norm. These districts are predominantly in cities, where "urban" is a euphemism used to refer to low-performing students of color and their teachers, who are assumed to need their instruction scripted in order to increase student performance. In these districts, administrators frantically search for that magic program that will save them from the penalties imposed as a result of the low performance on standardized tests of many of their students of color, a situation branded with the pernicious label "achievement gap." This label has exacerbated the cultural myth that the only way to close the gap is by focusing on weaknesses. As a result, we have been obsessively misdirected to turn our backs on the vast intellectual capacity of these students and to regard minimum proficiency as the ceiling, dismissing two inherent truths about learning as if they do not pertain to these individuals:

- All people have an intrinsic desire to learn and to be self-actualized. Maslow (1943) has shown that this desire is the human imperative.
- All brains are the same color. In other words, the way the brain makes learning happen does not differ from one culture to another. All brains require the enrichment opportunities to demonstrate and build strengths, supports to address weaknesses, strategies for developing critical thinking, and experiences that build the dispositions needed to be focused, engaged, tenacious, self-confident, and self-actualized. What is different among cultures is the information one is exposed to and the types of thinking processes that might be engaged in more often (Feuerstein, 1978; Feuerstein, Feuerstein, Falik, & Rand, 2006; Hilliard, 1977; Sternberg, 1998).

The myth about poor, urban students requiring the focus of their education to be their weaknesses is so robust, so spellbinding, that it has caused us to turn a blind eye to these truths, as well as to the most critically affecting reality regarding the achievement of these students: The disadvantagedness of students from poor, urban areas is that they are in fact school-dependent (Cooper, 2009). They enter kindergarten with the same unbridled excitement and effervescent enthusiasm as students from homes higher on the socioeconomic ladder, expecting to enjoy that promise pronounced to them by their parents: "In school you *will* learn." Their parents send them to school expecting that they will be provided with the enrichment, prerequisites, and opportunities they will need to learn, to achieve at high levels, and to measure up to the same standards as "other people's children." In fact, parents pay teachers the highest honor possible: They entrust their children and their children's success to them.

In spite of these truths about learning and the reality of the school-dependence of poor, urban students, the myth that perpetuates the focus on weaknesses drives the policies that replace enrichment with remediation and penalizing sanctions that incite fear—halting innovation and steering teachers toward uninspiring instruction. The result is a morass of disengagement that has stifled the motivation of the students who so desperately want to be pushed to what the poet David Whyte calls the "frontier of their intelligence" (Whyte, 2002, CD 1). The disengagement, in turn, has eroded the confidence and competence of thousands of teachers to inspire their students.

Yet there are thousands of other teachers in schools labeled as underperforming who have strategically built themselves islands of confidence and who work zealously—contrary to the demands of policies that prescribe narrow instruction—to engage their students in challenging, relevant curriculum that will push them to that intellectual "frontier" Whyte described. But instead of being recognized for their commitment or supported for eliciting students' growth (which the students can build on or see as an affirmation of their potential), these teachers are simply regarded as additional representatives of the negative traits with which their schools have been labeled. This kind of tagging has a devitalizing, negative effect on the motivation, initiative, and performance of principals, teachers, and their students, heinously propagating the underachievement that plagues urban districts.

Ending this plague will never come about through negative labels and sanctions. The powers that be must recognize that the debilitating effect of negative labeling and its repercussions is a sociological reality, one that has been cogently explained by David Whyte:

Since we have a society, a culture in America, that has privileged work above almost any other activity, we have created a culture in which our identities rely upon our work to an incredible degree. This is an enormous weight. . . . And you could be called many things in North America, many four-letter words, but the worst four-letter word is actually a five-letter word, which is "loser"—the name that says that you have in some way failed, failed at participating. And the great terror of this word, both for our personalities and for our souls is that it almost always carries the definition of other people's sense of winning, and so many ideas about work are contaminated by general, often surface ideas of what it means to win in the world. (Whyte, 2002, CD 4)

In urban areas the contamination is manifested as feelings of incompetence on the part of teachers and principals who have not fortified their own confidence. Their passion can dwindle to barely an ember, buried to the point that it flickers unnoticed—but it is still there. The ember never dies. It eternally seeks the oxygen of a new direction, one that can ignite creativity and passion once again.

IGNITING THE PEDAGOGY OF CONFIDENCE

I know that ember is there in the urban districts that reach out to my organization to assist them in reversing the seemingly endless flow of underachievement. We begin the rekindling process with teachers in these districts by opening staff development sessions with a question many have never been asked. This alien question is "What are the strengths of your students?" Many are disoriented by the question because it is so unexpected. However, after some reflection, they begin to enumerate the strengths of their students; strengths most often cited are being verbal, creative, expressive, analytical, resilient, and problem-solvers. The irony that emerges when we compare these lists of strengths with mandated achievement standards is that not only are the strengths the teachers have listed for their students targeted in their states' standards as being required for achievement, but they are also the same indicators used in identification surveys for admission into gifted and talented programs! This finding comes as a revelation for most of these teachers, so we move on to discuss *why* it is such a surprise. The discussion reveals that the cultural focus on weakness results in what is essentially an institutional authorization to ignore or undervalue the strengths already within these students—or, most daunting, the belief that the strengths are nonexistent.

What these teachers recognize from their own reflection is the impact the ideology of disbelief has on the purported intellectual capacity of school-dependent students. They realize that if the policies directing how to educate these students were based on an ideology of belief in their intellectual ability and potential, funding would cover identification of the strengths of the students—and strengths would in fact be found. This process of asking educators to focus on strengths is revitalizing, rekindling the embers of their passion and their belief that have been forced to smolder. Posing the question about student strengths is not a novel idea. It is the "secret invigorator" of teachers in "Gifted Land." When you truly believe in the intellectual potential of students, you start with the goal of identifying strengths and then provide enriching options and direction to bring those strengths to the surface and promote high intellectual performance as opposed to minimum proficiency. You provide enriching options because you know intuitively and through personal experience what Piaget proved so long ago: *High-level activities increase intellectual development* (Piaget, 1950).

Time after time I have witnessed teachers being stimulated by the identification of their students' strengths and the potential these strengths testify to, and, like teachers of students labeled as gifted, they are motivated to remember that this belief in potential is why they went into teaching. The challenge for these teachers once they remember this motivation and begin to focus on strengths is to stand up against the current deficit culture with confidence in their ability to inspire, elicit, and build on these strengths, enabling the high intellectual performance that encourages self-directed learning and self-actualization. This is the Pedagogy of Confidence®.

The Pedagogy of Confidence takes root in schools through structures single-mindedly focused on high intellectual performance for all students—structures that support and facilitate a high level of practice in every classroom. These structures are what I call mediative learning communities—communities in which all participants (teachers, principals, and students) are emancipated and empowered to share their voices to transform the school into an oasis where strengths are valued and self-directed learning is enabled. In mediative learning communities where the Pedagogy of Confidence thrives, efforts and practices emanate from a core belief in the innate and expansive intellectual capacity of students—*all* students—and in the latent and extensive pedagogical power of teachers—*all* teachers.

THE PEDAGOGY OF CONFIDENCE: A COOPERATIVE PROCESS

I have written this book with the intention of broadening the frame of reference for all who have influence on the destinies of our students—teachers, principals, superintendents, policymakers, parents, and community groups—with the hope that they will appreciate the fated reality that student motivation to learn is directly affected by teachers' confidence in their students' potential, concomitant with their own competence to nurture this potential. Teachers demonstrate their confidence in their students' capacity to learn through fearlessly articulating, supporting, and insisting upon the expectations that all of their students will learn. Teachers are enabled to act upon these expectations by confident principals who demonstrate indisputable belief in the capacity of their students and teachers, who guide and support teachers to identify and build on students' strengths, who provide opportunities for teachers to develop their craft and their voice, and who inspire teachers to inspire students.

The research that substantiates the theory behind the Pedagogy of Confidence is both old and new. The travesty is that the findings from this research about engaging and developing high intellectual performance have been either disregarded or limited to application for students labeled as gifted. However, if we are to reverse underachievement, this research must also inform our beliefs, our practices, and the structures we use to educate school-dependent students. This book describes the High Operational Practices gleaned from gifted education that fuel the Pedagogy of Confidence—practices that close the gap between students' potential and their achievement.

THE CONCEPTION AND INSTITUTIONALIZATION OF THE PEDAGOGY OF CONFIDENCE

The mentoring I have received from the eminent cognitive psychologist Reuven Feuerstein has inspired my conceptualization of the Pedagogy of Confidence. His belief in the vast intellectual capacity of all people, regardless of environmental condition or genetic predisposition, propelled his seminal research on the structural cognitive modifiability of the brain and the transformative effect that using specific cognitive strategies for mediating intelligence has on reversing underachievement. Feuerstein's research substantiates adopting the premise of gifted education as the philosophy of the Pedagogy of Confidence. This philosophy advocates the benefits of shifting the focus of instruction for school-dependent students from addressing their weaknesses to identifying and amplifying their intellectual potential and strengths, for engaging and accelerating learning and achievement.

Transforming the focus of American educational culture from one of deficit to one of belief in intellectual potential will not occur within the isolation of the classroom, where teachers are forced to operate on islands of confidence. Cultures are developed by shared belief in what is determined to be inherently relevant and meaningful to the group. Such a determination in the educational domain is generated by educational policy.

A redirected educational policy fueled by genuine belief in the intellectual capacity of all students could shift pedagogy toward an approach propelled by what Socrates argued was the real purpose of education: the drawing out of what is already inside the individual (Teacher's Mind Resources, n.d.). It is my hope that the research and experiences from the field shared in this book will drive educators to coalesce their power to influence change in the detrimental policies that pilot us away from the intellectual capital that resides within our urban students and away from the pedagogical promise of the teachers on whom they depend for nurturing this potential.

THE ORGANIZATION OF THE BOOK

This book is divided into three parts. It is designed to be a textual odyssey, navigating first through the evolution of the Pedagogy of Confidence. The journey continues with an examination of the cognitive and neuroscience research that substantiates the principles and High Operational Practices of the Pedagogy of Confidence. Finally, I present examples of the efforts of superintendents, principals, and teachers who earnestly strive to cultivate this pedagogy so they can manifest the promise of their school-dependent students and their commitment to those students.

Part I describes the beliefs, research, and experiences that inspired the genesis of the Pedagogy of Confidence. The discussion covers two important developments: (a) the evolution of the myth that fuels the instructional focus on weaknesses as the prescription for what the law calls low-performing students, and (b) the evolution of gifted education, as an illustration of how belief in student potential promulgates policies that dictate the trajectory of their success inside and outside of school. The review of both of these developments will include the impact of restrictive practices inside school and debilitating factors outside school that prevent school-dependent students from realizing their potential.

Part II presents the science of learning based on cognitive and neuroscience research that substantiates the intellectual development benefits of the High Operational Practices generated by the Pedagogy of Confidence. The discussion will place special focus on the groundbreaking theory and methodology of Reuven Feuerstein, whose work formed the foundation of the Pedagogy of Confidence. The High Operational Practices will be explained and illustrated through descriptions from Bridgeport (Connecticut) Public Schools; Greene County (Georgia) School System; Indianapolis Public Schools; Newark (New Jersey) Public Schools; and the San Francisco Unified School District. In these schools and districts, inspirational teachers have implemented High Operational Practices to propel their students to high intellectual performance. The role of dedicated and innovative super-intendents and principals in guiding the cultivation of the Pedagogy of Confidence will also be examined. In addition, the relationship of the High Operational Practices to Renzulli's Learning System® and the Thinking Maps® designed by David Hyerle will be described.

Part III pays special attention to the Mediative Learning Community, the preeminent structure vital to enabling the Pedagogy of Confidence. The conditions of a Mediative Learning Community that are conducive to cre-ating the transformative shared culture of staff and students needed to mitigate the effects of debilitating factors on the achievement of school-dependent students will be described. Examples will include descriptions of practices for empowering student investment in the Mediative Learning Community from Greene County, Newark Public Schools, and San Fran-cisco Unified Schools. In addition, the Pedagogical Flow Map—the struc-ture that creates a framework for translating the Pedagogy of Confidence into lesson or unit designs—will be illustrated.

I HAVE TAKEN THE OPPORTUNITY to use this book to target adolescents, with an elaborated focus on African American students. The reasons for the elaborated focus on African American students are twofold. First, as an Afri-can American myself, I bring a frame of reference that allows me to analyze and discuss the realities of these students from an acute, personal vantage point. Second, African Americans continue to be challenged by inequities in educational opportunities that impact their learning to the point that they are disproportionately referred to special education. Data from surveys by the Elementary and Middle Schools Technical Assistance Center verify that teachers and schools do in fact feel unprepared to meet the needs of "economically disadvantaged" students, with special education being per-ceived by many as the only resource available for helping students from this classification who are not succeeding. The referrals to special education are exacerbated by the sanctions imposed by test-driven accountability, which is compounded by prejudging and marginalizing programs, a reality that warrants drastic alteration (Elementary and Middle Schools Technical Assis-tance Center, n.d.).

My reasons for targeting adolescents are twofold as well. First, adoles-cence is a critical juncture educationally. For many this is the last opportu-nity for us as educators to exert the will to make the instructional choices that will determine the rest of our students' lives. That is, we can allow con-tinuation of the spiral of underachievement that relegates these students to failure or we can capitalize on their innate intellectual capacity. Second, adolescence is a critical juncture in the physiological, emotional, and cognitive development of students. It is a defining point for building both students' identity and their confidence in their own ability.

Neurobiology has illustrated that puberty can start as early as elementary school and can continue through the early twenties. This span across many years enables adolescents to master cultural knowledge through the extended observation of adult behavior that characterizes teaching and learning. We can capitalize on this developmental stage to steer students toward recognition of the culture associated with academic success. There are two caveats, however—and these are the goals this book addresses. The first is that the promise adolescence presents is contingent upon the provision of support with mediation to elicit the cognitive agility inherent in the formal operations students are capable of at this stage of cognitive development. The second caveat is that the cultural knowledge that is generated at the school—which these students are depending on for optimizing their intellectual capacities—cannot be limited to "other people's culture." For school-dependent students, school must be the oasis that inspires their learning to flourish. Such an oasis, or Mediative Learning Community, is generated by a culture that accommodates and assimilates the culture of the students themselves. Needless to say, a shared school culture inclusive of the culture of the students it serves is novel. This is a culture that requires belief that the intellectual capacity of school-dependent students has commerce, and therefore all would benefit from its cultivation. And that is what is needed—a transformed, shared culture that expects high intellectual performance from school-dependent students. This is the culture that animates the Pedagogy of Confidence.

INITIATING THE PEDAGOGY OF CONFIDENCE

As you read this book I ask you to remember what drew you to learning as a student and why you wanted to become a teacher. Then channel the passion you had to turn this memory into practices that would elicit your students' desire to learn and your own ability to nurture their potential to achieve. This remembering is in fact the first key to the Pedagogy of Confidence. These memories are our own personal empirical research, our own primary resources. They are the deep-rooted, first-hand knowledge about learning that is often more valuable and valid than the knowledge of those who write tomes of research after watching others teach. When you remember and act on your personal "primary resource" and hearken to your passion, the choices you make about effective learning strategies can have a dramatic impact on your ability to elicit high intellectual performance from your students. You will once again be able to experience the glow of competence and confidence that sparked your belief in your ability to elicit and support the potential of underachieving students for high intellectual performance.

This "glow" of the memories of confidence and competence is not just a fleeting, feel-good stroll down memory lane. The glow you feel is actually a neurological response that affects your very being. Eric Jensen (1998, pp. 32–34) explains the reason for the internal glow that results from remembering the competence and confidence associated with the impact of our ability to elicit high intellectual performance in students. Confidence acquired from competence causes us to become intensely stimulated. This stimulation causes a burning of glucose, which results in our brain "glowing" from the energy of the glucose that is consumed. The stimulation is actually acting like a brain "nutrient," making us feel stronger. For teachers, demonstrations of student learning and success resulting from our teaching serve as feedback to us about our choices. This feedback is a great asset, because it fuels us with both a deep sense of competence and a sense of being valued. This sense of competence and being valued releases neurotransmitters of pleasure—endorphins—which help us enjoy our work more. When feelings of competence are increased, fewer catecholamines (the body's natural chemical response to stress) are released. The effect of competence on the body is the same whether we are actively engaged in these experiences or just remembering them.

For those of you who are confident about your capacity to address the intelligence and deep potential of underachieving students, I hope this book will provide you with the ammunition to confirm and strengthen your conviction. For those of you who feel so weary from the battle against the shackles of policies that mandate the negative focus on weaknesses that your belief has been minimized to embers so weak you no longer feel the glow, I hope this book rekindles those embers so you believe again in your ability to unlock the immense potential of your school-dependent students. Finding the combination of interactions to unlock it requires an ardent belief in this potential, the desire to try all means to tap it, and the courage to connect to the students through what we all value most for our self-actualization: competence and confidence. When we feel this competence and confidence, we inspire it in our students. We explore the endless opportunities for creating the bridges that confidence provides. These bridges allow students to see connections and relationships between their world and the world we are trying to open to them. We provide the motivation to pursue the dreams of success that all these students harbor.

SO, EXPERIENCE THE GLOW and remember:

- Remember what it was about you that made you feel you had something to offer students to help them learn. What was that something?
- Remember that first year of teaching and the hope that generated your desire to reach students. What did that motivate you to do?
- Remember your first concrete evidence of success and how it tweaked your passion and emboldened you to use your gifts to unlock the gifts in your students. What were those gifts you acted on?
- Remember the students for whom you had the most profound impact. How did you engage them? What did it feel like when you realized you had in fact made an impact?
- Remember your strengths, your skills, your attributes, your passion.

These gifts, strengths, skills, attributes, and passion are still there. They make you the one the students have been waiting for.

PART I

The Belief

1

The Need to Believe

Change the input and the brain changes accordingly.
—Reuven Feuerstein

What is the genesis of the Pedagogy of Confidence?

The Pedagogy of Confidence is fearless expectation and support for all students to demonstrate high intellectual performance. It is based on the transformative belief that within all of us resides an untapped reservoir of potential to achieve at high levels. When teachers operate from a Pedagogy of Confidence they have no doubt about the potential of their school-dependent students or about their own ability to elicit and guide the application of this potential. They transmit to their students their belief that the students will be productive contributors to society by providing what Lisa Delpit (1995) calls the "Codes of Power" that will enable the students to act on this belief about their potential.

When teachers are supported to operate from a Pedagogy of Confidence, they switch their instructional focus from what must be taught to how to maximize learning, artfully using the science of learning to create a "gifted" education that focuses on cultivating student strengths while providing the High Operational Practices that inspire high intellectual performance. The artfulness of the pedagogy is manifested in the way teachers confidently enable students to make personal connections to their learning, affirming the value of their lived experiences. Confident teachers do this by using the interconnectedness of culture, language, and cognition as a frame to:

- Conduct their teaching methods
- Choreograph the integration of enrichment to identify and direct strengths and interests
- Compose and orchestrate learning strategies to engage participation, ensure understanding, and address needs
- Engineer the design of assessments to engage, expand, and accelerate the learning of their urban students (Jackson, 2001)

The uncompromising aim of this Pedagogy of Confidence is to empower teachers and their students with the voice and the competence to realize two outcomes: self-directed learning and self-actualization.

My years of observing the high intellectual performance demonstrated by the school-dependent students I taught in the urban trenches of Yonkers, New York, along with my experiences as the Director of Gifted Programs for the New York City Public Schools, provoked me to infuse understandings from gifted education to codify a pedagogy aimed at eclipsing the prejudice about the intelligence of school-dependent students and the power of their teachers to cultivate this intelligence. I have spent more than 30 years in this process, but the final articulation of the Pedagogy of Confidence was inspired by David Whyte's (2002) description of the poetic process as an enabling vehicle to express our deepest insights clearly and courageously. He talks of developing the confidence to encourage those who need inspiration to explore the frontiers of their potential. His description of poetry can be paraphrased by substituting teachers, students, and principals, and the context in which we work as urban educators. This reformulation elucidates the role of the Pedagogy of Confidence in following our moral compass and emancipating our competence to keep our promise to our urban students, who depend on us to identify, nurture, and unleash their inherent intellectual capacities:

> There is a miraculousness of personal transformation that only happens when you bravely look back and feel the fragility and the insight in what you know to be your personal truth or "moral compass." When you are brave enough to move from this truth, you use a bold voice to stand up and articulate what you know to be right and just. . . . It allows us the freedom to articulate the truth about our beliefs. It emancipates us to change our perspective, remembering, rediscovering, and re-imagining our confidence in our ability to speak in a bold voice for those who have no voice—the courage to inspire students to explore and actualize the frontier of their intelligence. (Whyte, 2002, CD 1)

The Pedagogy of Confidence is my personal truth—a truth substantiated by the transformation of students and teachers I have had the privilege of witnessing through long-term relationships and supported by the findings of both cognitive and neuroscience research. Whyte's (2002) concept of "using a bold voice" compelled me to write this book in hopes of countering what Reuven Feuerstein identifies as a cognitive holocaust that continues to decimate urban districts, ravaging the lives of both students and teachers, robbing them of the opportunity for self-actualization. Conceptualizing "my truth" and the synthesis of my personal experiences with the evolution of the science of learning is best narrated through a diary-like account of my urban odyssey.

THE PAST

The late 1960s and early '70s were a time of great dissonance outside and inside of urban schools. Outside schools young people were rebelling against the government that had engaged us in the Vietnam War. Each day, male friends of mine waited fearfully to see if their number would be drawn in a lottery that would determine if they would be sent to risk their lives on battlefields fighting a people the U.S. government had determined needed to be controlled.

Inside urban schools a different kind of dissonance was taking place—one I was experiencing firsthand in the school in which I was teaching. This was the heyday of the Elementary and Secondary Education Act (ESEA; enacted in 1965), which allotted monetary assistance for the development of compensatory education programs designed to identify and remediate what were considered "weaknesses" of students designated as "disadvantaged" under a funding scheme called "Title I." The test scores of students who fell below the statewide Normal Curve Equivalency on norm-referenced tests were considered illustrative of cognitive deficiencies (Ginsburg, 1972; Levine & Bane, 1975), and students deemed to be affected by environmental conditions caused by poverty were classified as disadvantaged. The inevitable result of this approach to classification (correlating low scores on standardized tests with cognitive deficiencies) was the prejudging of the intelligence of these students. Battles ensued between the supporters and the critics of the educational policies that engineered the classifications that resulted in this prejudging, which translated into "low-level instruction" absent of enrichment for the students judged to be deficient (Ginsburg, 1972). The battles wound up in courtrooms, where it was determined through analysis of the construction of the standardized tests used to determine student classification that the tests could not make predictions about the potential of "disadvantaged" students (*Hobson v. Hansen*, 1967; *Larry P. v. Riles*, 1984; *Slade v. Board of Education of Hartford County*, 1958). However, a catalyst for focusing on weaknesses had been put into play through ESEA, which generated policy deeming that schools identified as having a majority of students classified as disadvantaged and underachieving would be eligible for financial assistance. The repercussions of the economic reality we are experiencing today were similarly felt at that time, and the need districts had for monetary support fueled the inclination the administrators (at the state, district, and school levels) had to ignore the findings of the courts and create programs that concentrated on weak areas of performance as the norm for poor, underachieving students in order to obtain additional funding to save, if not merely buoy, their instructional programs. Those who succumbed to the temptation of receiving additional funding helped institutionalize the myth of cognitive deficiencies being the appropriate and necessary focus for educating poor, underachieving students. This inculcated belief in the ideology that generated the policy. To be both cost-effective and reflective of the new ideology, ESEA declared the efficacy of supplementing the existing core curriculum with remediation techniques for a narrow range of school-related skills, instead of creating a totally new curriculum for the labeled "minority" population. As a result, remedial programs were implemented in a "pull-out" design (Reisner, 1980) that removed students from the standard instruction taking place within their classrooms.

As programs began to proliferate, standardized achievement tests became the sole diagnostic tool for judging the effectiveness of the remedial pre-scriptions. The prescriptive teaching methods in turn became less and less varied and more and more narrow, reflecting the "connexionist theory," which stated that the way to prevent students from repeating errors was by interpreting the errors and then instructing the students how to respond— by having them experience the connection of the error to reaction and reward. The result was the imposition of repeated tasks void of interest or meaning to students (Collins, 1961, p. 104).

The remedial programs that reflected the policies related to Title I were the antithesis of the educational training I received. I, like many other teach-ers who were rebelling against the pervasive marginalizing ideology, was the product of Open Classroom education, a system that ran counter to the educational philosophy that ESEA promoted. An "open classroom" was defined as a student-centered classroom that functioned within a school built without interior walls. The objective was to facilitate flexible organiza-tion of various groupings for learning (similar to the way differentiated instruction is organized today). I was trained to guide students to achieve their assigned learning goals through a combination of small-group work and customized "contracts" that directed them to move at their own pace through enriching resources and activities that were set up in a variety of learning centers in the open space.

I had the great fortune to work with the same group of students from 3rd through 5th grades within this pedagogical design. Our school was in a "low-income" neighborhood in which 85% of the students were African American and 15% were Puerto Rican, most of whom came from environ-ments affected by poverty. I believed deeply in the intellectual capacities of these students, a belief affirmed every day by their monumental growth and the brilliance that shone in spite of the environmental conditions in which they found themselves. My 4th- and 5th-graders were diagramming sentences, doing algebra and trigonometry, and composing short stories worthy of formal publishing. I believed in them and, more importantly, they believed in their own capacity. In spite of the affirming results I was privileged to experience in this open classroom environment, the limiting controls promulgated by Title I began to impact our principal, steering her into the restrictive, low-level world of remedial reading and mathematics instruction. This is when a disorienting dissonance and my quiet rebellion began.

During this time I collaborated with teammates to put our most creative effort forward through our enriching learning centers. Our plans became increasingly derailed as the principal began instituting remedial pull-out programs. I began witnessing the nightmare experienced in thousands of schools across the country today: Several of my students who were being exposed within our class to a variety of tasks that engaged and motivated self-directed learning through their learning contracts were being pulled out to be subjected to content in basal readers that consisted of tasks and materials with which middle-class students were more familiar (Orem, 1967); subject matter that was too distant from their experience (Ginsburg, 1972); and stories that generated disinterest, which exacerbated their underachievement (Ginsburg, 1972). The pull-out format instituted to supposedly foster individualized attention became problematic in that it stigmatized and isolated students and bred discontinuities in instruction (i.e., few lessons were jointly prepared by both the remedial and the classroom teachers). Improvements observed by the remedial teacher were not reflected in the regular classwork. Because Title I programs were understaffed, pull-out programs were overpopulated. Students were expected to work independently on worksheets of exercises as the remedial teacher circulated. Those who encountered problems were left waiting for assistance, inhibiting their individual progress (Ginsburg, 1972, p. 200).

The major atrocity of the remedial programs was acutely apparent during the 3 years I taught the same students. As described in studies of Title I children around the country, I saw performance in reading for numerous students who were pulled out of my class begin to decrease (Hilliard, 1977). The cumulative deficit in reading was crucially consequential, for it caused a traumatic ripple effect in total school performance because achievement in most subjects was so dependent then (and now) on facility in reading.

The principal of the school who established the pull-out program was sincerely committed to our students. Her support of the open classroom design reflected a belief in a pedagogy that recognized the benefit of engaging students in enriching resources and self-directed learning. Yet she was compelled to adhere to a policy that coalesced reading instruction around a narrow, limiting perspective that the basal reader was the sole vehicle to ensure the "proper teaching of reading" and remediation was the answer to addressing areas of weaknesses, a perspective that ignored the broader understanding of the learning process and how to enable and intensify it. This oppression—this narrow perspective related to educating school-dependent students that animated Title I programs—began to restrict her pedagogical direction, in turn repressing my instructional choices. The height of this oppression came when I was the subject of a "pop-in" observation during a social studies lesson. The principal called me in to meet with her later that afternoon, stating that although the lesson was engaging and strong, it had occurred during the reading period, when "teaching content" was not allowed. I began to feel friction on both a visceral and an intellectual level between the practices of open education, which facilitated growth of my students when they were guided through enriching resources that enabled them to investigate, and the suffocating limitations of the prescriptive practices spawned by the focus on weaknesses. The friction caused a state of internal dissonance that kept me off-center as I tried to reconcile what I had studied, my own empirical research emerging from observations of my students over time, and the repercussions being experienced by my students relegated to the pull-out program. This dissonance fueled a rebellion through which I was able to garner the confidence to confront the principal. I presented my case, articulating how social studies and science provided content with which to engage learning and facilitate the teaching and application of reading skills. The principal's resistance to my argument induced me to escalate. I challenged her to agree to allow me to teach reading through content areas if I could demonstrate to her the validity of my argument through lessons she would observe. Before she observed the lesson, I would meet with her and specifically identify the reading skills I would be able to teach and the levels of comprehension my students would attain. Having witnessed the engagement of my students and their continuous growth during the year and a half I had been their teacher at that point, she allowed me to substantiate my case—which I did.

From that time, the principal accepted my teaching reading in the content areas as my instructional approach in lieu of the prescribed basal program. The reality is that if I had not had the confidence to rebel through a cogently pled argument, the restrictive, prescriptive reading and math blocks of 90 minutes each would have continued to eliminate opportunities for my students to deeply explore and learn social studies or science, leaving them "undereducated" and with a restricted frame of reference.

THE IMPETUS FOR SETTING WEAKNESSES AS THE FOCUS OF INSTRUCTION FOR SCHOOL-DEPENDENT STUDENTS

Control Versus Direction

It was at this point in my teaching career that I had an epiphany about the battle that was being waged in urban schools between policies that provided direction for growth versus policies that imposed control (a distinction that sounds familiar today as well, no doubt). What I gleaned from observing my students in the open classroom environment was that learning resulted from directed actions that reflected belief in student potential and promoted growth of that potential. My students' self-directed learning patterns were a result of the enriching instructional resources I had been furnishing them. Such direction—based on belief in potential—was positive and constructive. It amplified, maximized, and optimized the intellectual ability of the students. What I realized about the prescriptive practices that were spawned by policies that mandated control was that they were driven by a *lack* of belief either in students or in teachers, or most often both. These controls arrested or inhibited actions that could generate learning. Such control was negative in the way in which it deconstructed or destroyed inspiring, engaging instruction, causing disengagement, arrested growth, or even growth that atrophied, leaving students perpetually disenfranchised. I knew that I was correct in my perception about the impact of policies (and their concomitant programs) that mandated control. The proof was everywhere—in the artifacts of students' low achievement that littered the educational landscape we were witnessing. The potent impact of the control policies became so anchored in that landscape that it prevails to this day.

Control Through Classification

The prejudging practice of sorting students based on standardized criteria evolved from the government's need to expedite and facilitate classifying students without the expense of training teachers to assess the learning potential of the students. Education became the only field in which requirements or mandates were not followed by explicit training based on research about the stated objective—reversing underachievement (Hilliard, 1977; Noguera, 2003). This governmental practice of control through classification of students set off development of a chain of marginalizing labels that fostered misperceptions about students, in turn perpetuating a cycle of prejudicing belief and low expectations.

The marginalizing labels for classifying students included:

* *Minority* (versus students of color, stating an ethnicity, or no classification)
* *Low-achiever* (versus underachiever)
* *Disadvantaged* (versus school-dependent)

To appreciate how such labels tainted the perceptions of educators then—and still do today—consider the associations each label began to engender and the deep, harmful message each one has sent through the years.

Minority versus students of color or no classification. When a Congressman or Congresswoman is identified as the "Minority Leader of the House," the implication is that this person is from the party without the power. When an individual is classified as a minority, the same implication applies: less power. The marginalizing result this term has generated is that persons of color have been classified as a minority even when they are in environments where they are literally the majority of the population. As a person of multiracial heritage, I have been classified as a minority—regardless of the number of generations my ancestors have been here and the various racial groups from which they came. I have personally felt (and felt for my students) the psychological and limiting impact such a term generates. Two realities regarding the classification of people with any African ancestry became more pronounced early in my career: (a) choosing any term to describe us would continue to impose an inexact, man-made classification, with potentially volatile backlash; and (b) there would arise an explosive inquiry into and revolt against the pernicious reasons such a classification was employed at all. Numerous justifications for the classification could be cited, but the result remained (and still remains) the same: the implication of minority as meaning "less than"—forever a classification as well as a destination, as further explicated by the following labels.

Low-achiever versus underachiever. The term "low-achiever" has incited prejudices regarding the potential of students by implying that a student has attained the maximum ability of which he or she is capable. The choice of terminology has indicated expectations and possibilities or the lack thereof. However, the reality I observed was that the students who came to me plagued by low test scores were *under*achievers. Their test scores were not indicative of their maximum ability. As they were exposed to enriching experiences and supported by strategies that developed their skills, their intellectual ability flourished.

Disadvantaged versus school-dependent. As cited earlier, the term "disadvantaged" from the ESEA authorization referred to environmental conditions caused by low socioeconomic status. The proposition was that lack of money hindered students from being exposed to what were considered "cultural" experiences needed to construct and infer meaning in the academic setting. Those "mainstream" cultural experiences were Eurocentric experiences (e.g., exposure to achievements in the classical arts), and lacking exposure to those experiences resulted in the students being considered "disadvantaged." The terminology underscored the implication that the ethnic or personal culture of students classified as "minority" was not only considered irrelevant to learning, it was generally regarded as inferior. The debilitating result of this implication has been that "minority" has become synonymous with "disadvantaged." Equally as debilitating has been the manner in which the potential of these students has been assessed. Contrary to the reasoning behind the classification of "disadvantaged" (recognition that poverty limits range of exposure), the potential of students affected by poverty has been assessed as if they were being exposed to the same enriching experiences their more advantaged peers enjoyed thanks to family economics. The ignored reality has been that poor, urban students have been school-dependent—that is, they have been dependent on school to provide the enrichment needed to achieve on the standardized tests. The remedial programs and prescriptive practices instituted in the 1970s excluded such enrichment in order to make more time for remedial drills. What was also ignored—but what I knew personally—was that the culture of these students was replete with a heritage of strength and accomplishment that could be used to bolster self-confidence and create powerful bridges to the concepts they had to explore for academic achievement.

THIS PATHOLOGY of ascribing marginalizing terms that started in the 1970s has persisted with the introduction of an additional marginalizing label that has arrested pedagogical practice: "disabled" (the literal translation being "not able"). This term has become synonymous with minority as well, as evidenced by the fact that the majority of students in special education are African American males.

These terms are all examples of what is considered "positional language," meaning that such language indicates a position of "power over" individuals instead of "power with" individuals (Delpit, 1995; Hilliard, 1991/1995; Mahiri, 1998). These marginalizing, prejudicing terms spawned by the policies of control that arose out of Title I classification precipitated a series of limiting realities for school-dependent students of color.

THE LIMITING REALITY OF ASSESSMENT PRACTICES

Alfred Binet pioneered targeting weaknesses through the use of standardized forms of testing in the 1940s. It was his intention, however, to make a genuine "effort to help rather than limit the prospects of those who were different and especially of those children who had difficulty learning in the normal classroom" (Samuda, 1998, p.1). Binet's premise was that one could assess an individual's mental age through comparison with the average performance of other individuals. However, the mental measure that Binet had intended for use in research went quickly into general application. An initial general application of his premise of mental age became the basis for Wilhelm Stern's creation of a formula that was used to designate an intelligence quotient (proportion or percentage) derived from Binet-type tests that were classified as intelligence tests and were used for various purposes. This formula was computed as:

$$IQ = 100 \times \frac{MA}{CA}$$

That is, IQ was calculated to be 100 times an individual's mental age (MA), which is determined by comparing his or her performance to the average performance of others on that test, divided by his or her chronological age (CA) (Wilson, 1978). Instead of facilitating the design of instruction to specifically address the needs identified from the tests, the results were used for making public policy that resulted in sorting students. This practice launched the bell curve mentality. The sorting inspired the need to demonstrate that curriculum would be different for the various groups, with high performance on the tests generating more rigorous, enriched curriculum. To validate this need to have more rigorous curriculum for those who scored higher on the IQ test, many pursuits were undertaken to clarify or justify conceptions related to exceptional abilities. More IQ tests were designed specifically to measure the intelligence of children. The mental abilities targeted because of the value placed on them in academics were (and still are) in the areas of verbal acuity, reasoning, number facility, and space conceptualization.

Theory at the time of the development of IQ tests postulated that an individual's intelligence was constant and unalterable. Longitudinal tests had not been executed to validate whether this in fact was true, so myths validating the beliefs about intelligence developed, substantiating sorting and the creation of specialized programs. IQ tests gained utility because they were standardized to assess large groups of students. The standardization process was a result of designing the tests based on the frame of reference of the majority of students, as indicated by Binet. This majority was considered the "norm." Therefore, the items on the IQ norm-referenced tests were (and still are) specific to the culture of the students who composed the majority population. The result was that students who were culturally different from those against whom the tests were normed scored much lower on the IQ tests. (This practice of norm-referencing is the same basis upon which textbooks and curriculum are designed. This explains why an IQ test can determine how well students will do in school. If you are part of the norm group, your frame of reference reflects the kinds of examples used on the tests as well as in the curriculum [Sternberg, 1998].) The recognition of culture-specific items on the IQ test resulted in the test being considered by many as culturally biased.

The use of IQ for sorting occurred during the height of the segregation era, so the poor performance of African American students was sanctioned as reflective of low intelligence and responded to by the creation of segregated programs, tracking, inferior curriculum, and the acceptance of low expectations for the success of these students. The original intent of Binet to diagnose learning and create appropriate and successful prescriptions to ameliorate learning and achievement was upended through use of the test as a tool for sorting and denying the level of education necessary to achieve high degrees of academic and personal success.

My response to my epiphany—my recognition that it was an ideology of weakness that mandated control at the expense of practices that directed growth—was to research policy based on an ideology of nurturing strengths that directed growth. With each succeeding year, my students demonstrated a rate of growth that defied the myth of the ideology of weakness and the concomitant prejudice about the ability of such students. I pledged myself to finding policies that would direct the design of pedagogy in ways that would ensure the inclusion of experiences that activate, elicit, and nurture the potential of my students. I wanted to learn what distinguished such policies and substantiated the associated practices. What I discovered was that at the very same time that policies mandating a focus on weaknesses were proliferating for students labeled as "disadvantaged," other policies were being enacted for students who were labeled "gifted" that entitled them to pedagogy that would identify and nurture their strengths. The proliferation of the myths regarding intelligence had precipitated the bell curve mentality and the prejudice it engendered, reserving policies that directed growth and opportunities for self-actualization for those advantaged few. This reality only reinforced my resolve. Thus, I began an analysis of the specific practices that were employed when students were labeled as gifted and infused them into my pedagogy to ensure that I would propel the potential of my students into fruition.

GIFTED PROGRAMS:
THE CULTURE OF BELIEF AND HIGH EXPECTATIONS

"Gifted" programs originally surfaced in the educational terrain during the early 1960s in response to Russia's launch of Sputnik 1 (the world's first Earth-orbiting artificial satellite). The need to compete with Russia for dominance in science and mathematics produced a belief in the functionality of specialized programs to nurture particular expertise in these fields. This interest spurred many educational researchers to devise empirical studies to investigate tools for assessing the aptitude of students who might be considered to have "exceptional" abilities in order to better cultivate their development into "gifted" scientists. To promote this endeavor, the federal government designated five categories of giftedness (creative or productive thinking, the visual or performing arts, leadership, academic aptitude, and general intellectual ability) so that monetary support could be allotted. My search for the strategies used in these programs to elicit and develop abilities led me to determine that the most critical ingredients of pedagogy for those labeled gifted were belief and high expectations. These high expectations motivated teachers (and still do) to seek strategies and opportunities that focused on strengths and interests—strategies that engaged and challenged cognitive skills and higher intellectual performance. I also discovered that this pedagogy of gifted education was designed to reflect the actual etymological Latin base of the term education, "*educo*," which means to draw out one's potential (Teacher's Mind Resources, n.d.).

My passion for teaching had guided me to recognize what education should be about. My experiences with my students had verified what high expectations and appropriate support could nurture. And countering the reality of the endless underperformance of students when weaknesses are the focus set the course of the research I would undertake—research that became my doctoral dissertation. The hypothesis of my dissertation was my reality: In the pool of students labeled as underachievers there is the propensity for high intellectual performance. I began my search for the theories that would substantiate my belief and provide explanation beyond my empirical experiences for why my students could demonstrate gifted behaviors when so many thousands like them probably had gifts that remained undemonstrated. The work of Joseph Renzulli offered an answer to my query. Based on research findings gleaned from years of studying individuals labeled as gifted, Renzulli determined that a significant feature of these individuals was that their giftedness was neither always manifested nor was it obvious in every area of their lives. In fact, his findings (as well as those of others, more recently including Colvin, 2008, and Gladwell, 2008) revealed that there have been few gifted people such as Paul Robeson or Leonardo da Vinci, who demonstrated giftedness in multiple areas. Instead, most individuals labeled as gifted demonstrated this giftedness at certain times, under certain conditions, and in certain situations (Renzulli, 1978). This recognition steered Renzulli's identification of the common traits of individuals labeled as gifted. These traits included above-average ability, task commitment, and creativity. However (and this is key to his research), he discovered that these three traits were not manifested in everything gifted individuals did, but rather appeared in relation to things that they had a passionate interest in—interest that when guided evolved into exceptional strengths or "gifts." Renzulli has shown that it is in fact recognition of this relationship that generated what has classically been stated as the two purposes of gifted programs: (a) to provide young people with maximum opportunities for self-fulfillment through the development and expression of one or a combination of performance areas where superior potential may be present, and (b) to increase society's supply of persons who will help to solve the problems of contemporary civilization by becoming producers of knowledge and art rather than mere consumers of existing information. Renzulli's findings were proof of the power of policy that authorized the direction of growth—the policy of gifted education.

The undeniable reality for me was that provision of "maximum opportunities for self-fulfillment" in gifted programs is what nurtures the traits that generate the demonstration of strengths or "giftedness." In other words, gifted behavior or high intellectual performance is developed when strategies and opportunities are provided that bridge learning to interests and abilities, elicit gifted behaviors and habits of mind, expose students to content that builds their frames of reference and engages exploration, support development of the requisite skills to strengthen cognition and enable self-directed learning, and provide opportunities for the application of learning in authentic and meaningful ways. As I reviewed these purposes and practices associated with gifted programs, one question arose that would steer my research: What happens when these are the goals for all students?

Once again, Renzulli's work answered the question for me. He translated his findings regarding the experiences that nurture the traits conducive to the development of giftedness into an instructional design he labeled the Schoolwide Enrichment Model. Through the implementation of this model he demonstrated the catalyzing effects such experiences had in eliciting gifted behavior in students previously performing along the full continuum of standardized achievement test results (Renzulli & Reis, 2007).

In summary, what I extracted from Renzulli's research about programs designed to develop gifted behaviors was that the pedagogy these programs espoused targeted confidence—of both teachers and students—as the operative goal. I realized that it was confidence that was the foundation for high expectations and the focus on strengths, possibilities, new creations, and new meaning for students. Confidence advanced exploration, discovery, self-direction, multiple frames for thinking and acting, and the development and application of new knowledge and skills. Confidence was empowering, pushing cognition to deeper levels of existence and expression (Jackson & Davis, 2009). It was this foundation of gifted pedagogy that motivated me to isolate what I recognized as "low-focus/high-impact considerations" from gifted pedagogy. I characterized these features in this way because they are the considerations that received low focus in the development of general pedagogy (and were virtually ignored in the development of instruction or "programs" for poor, underachieving students) and yet had been incorporated into gifted pedagogy because they had proven to have high impact in engaging learning and developing performance or products valued as demonstrative of high intellectual ability. These low-focus/high-impact considerations had been highlighted in the gifted education classes I was pursuing as being substantiated by cognitive science for their ability to expand intellectual abilities. The effects of these practices are now verified by research in neuroscience that I will discuss in Part II of this book (Caine & Caine, 2006; Feuerstein, 1979a; Gardner, 1983/2003; Hattie, 2009; Hilliard, 1991/1995; Jensen, 1998; Sternberg, 1998; Sylwester, 2007).

Knowing the capacity of my students firsthand, it was easy to surmise that such considerations would intensify and nurture that capacity, so they became the beacons for my pedagogy. These low-focus/high-impact considerations included:

- Identifying and activating student strengths
- Eliciting high intellectual performance
- Providing enrichment
- Integrating prerequisites

I also capitalized on two additional considerations I recognized to be paramount for engaging and amplifying the intellectual capacity of my school-dependent students of color: building relationships and creating bridges from what must be taught to the lived experiences of these students. Both of these considerations demonstrated to the students the value I placed on who they were and the lives they had outside our classroom. I strived to have them appreciate the importance of the reciprocal relationship necessary to make our classroom an oasis in which they felt they could confidently grow.

The intellectual growth of my students was manifested in their inquiring minds, their thirst for learning, and their demonstration of exceptional performance in a variety of areas. These manifestations intensified my resolve to join the tumultuous educational battle against the dark forces of policy that perpetrated the disregard of the boundless potential of students like mine and obviated the experiences that could cultivate this potential. The fact that one of the stated purposes of gifted programs was then (and is still today) the development of superior potential that *"may be present"* was especially antagonizing to me because that stipulation should apply to all students. My escalating fervor was the catalyst for development of the Pedagogy of Confidence and the low-focus/high-impact considerations that would later be formalized as the High Operational Practices of this pedagogy.

2

The Continuing Drama of Disregarded Realities

*A prediction, in a field where prediction is not possible,
is no more than a prejudice.*   —Malcolm Gladwell

---

*What current realities are antagonistic to the
Pedagogy of Confidence?*

I have had the opportunity to experience the metamorphosis of urban education from several informative vantage points: classroom teacher, Director of Gifted Programs and Executive Director of Instruction and Professional Development for the largest school system in the United States, adjunct professor, and now Chief Executive Officer for the National Urban Alliance for Effective Education (NUA). From these vantage points I have witnessed a battle of beliefs about how to educate underachieving school-dependent students of color between those who subscribe to the weaknesses-based approach and those who champion a strengths-based/directed-growth pedagogy. Those who are antagonistic toward a strengths-based strategy are disregarding two critical realities: (a) the reciprocal relationship between teacher confidence and student success, and (b) the impact of the students' experiences outside and inside of school on their motivation, intellectual development, and learning.

INCITING FEAR (FALSE EVIDENCE APPEARING REAL): PERPETUATING THE MYTH

During the course of the 25 years that preceded my recognition of the benefits of gifted education for stimulating intellectual development and learning for all students, funding allotted for "restricted" gifted programs continued to reflect belief in the intellectual capacity of an anointed few, supporting the aim of fostering strengths and intellectual development in these students. In the same period, programs generated from Title I funds and designed for poor, underachieving students continued to reflect a *lack* of belief in the capacity of these students, focusing instead on identifying and targeting weaknesses, perpetuating the myth that had originated 30 years earlier. The lack of achievement of these Title I students as they were shepherded through programs reflective of the myth grew to epidemic proportions, seeming to substantiate the fixed mind-set many had about the limitations of the intellectual capacity of urban students. Instead, the undeniable reality about these programs was that the focus on weaknesses never worked (Dweck, 2000). In fact, the cognitive and neuroscience research regarding learning that began to surface during this period demonstrated that the weaknesses-based approach was the antithesis of what was needed to stimulate learning. But the ideology was so entrenched that it transcended the research as well as test data that gave glaring proof of the failure of the practices and structures mandated or promulgated through Title I. Performance of Title I children in reading actually slowed, stagnated, or decreased as they proceeded through school (Hilliard, 1977). Turning a blind eye to the evidence regarding the cause of the underachievement, Congress enacted yet another control policy—a pernicious iteration called No Child Left Behind (NCLB). I call it a pernicious iteration because the fallout from this policy is even more toxic than what came before. The mandated programs of NCLB have produced the same dismal results of stagnated or decreased achievement of students as were seen with most Title I instructional practices (Hess & Henig, 2008; National Center for Fair & Open Testing, 2008; Yatvin, 2003), creating a perception that has metastasized into the cancer now framed as the "achievement gap." This concept has been so toxic that it has catalyzed a correlation between underachievement and race, steering us away from the reality of the situation. An appreciation of the breadth of all students' intellectual capacity should motivate us to recognize and address what is in fact the real gap school-dependent students have been relegated to experience: the gap between their potential and their achievement.

The fallout of this misperception of the correlation between achievement and race has been an almost insurmountable predisposition toward prejudging the intellectual potential of poor, underachieving students. This phenomenon can be blatantly prevalent in urban districts, where 73% of the teachers identify themselves as white or racially and culturally different from their students (Mahiri, 1998). In these districts, where teachers are under all kinds of pressure, the stressor they articulate the most emotionally to us in NUA professional development sessions is fear—fear about their inability to prepare their students for the tests they must take; fear about their inability to translate standards and assessments into instruction; and, most poignantly, fear about their inability to reach their culturally different students who are labeled as being representative of that devaluing phenomenon called the "achievement gap" (Jackson, 2001).

2010: THE TUMULTUOUS BATTLE

I shudder at what has become the legacy of the stereotyping beliefs, practices, and structures promulgated by control policies in urban education. The tumultuous battle over how to educate underachieving school-dependent students continues to escalate, with the dark forces of marginalizing, incapacitating control policies taking on a virulent new identity. In this iteration, control is framed as "turnaround," and "turnaround funds" are appropriated for "turning around" troubled schools. The cancer has mutated to produce new forms of control that either eliminate personnel (replacing at least 50% of a school's existing staff, called "turnaround"), dismantle existing structures (turning a school over to a charter operation or an outside manager through a practice called the "restart" process, or entirely closing schools and transferring students through arbitrary placements), or deconstruct programs (providing professional development and coaching to teachers based on the same old ideology, and making changes to curriculum, instruction, and teacher evaluation through practices dubbed "transformation"). The Federal rules are structured in a way that encourages adoption of the "turnaround" or "restart" options, the most controlling approaches (Maxwell, 2010).

These iterations of control policies have made something painfully clear to me: Urban education has not evolved. It has devolved. One need only look back on the previous approaches and their incapacitating effect to arrive at the sad prognosis for the next stage of this cancer: expansion of the cognitive holocaust that perpetuates prejudice about the intellectual capacity of school-dependent students and destruction of the confidence of the many unheralded teachers who have in fact elicited exponential growth from their students despite prejudicing policies.

Ignored Consequences Reiterated

I do not believe that all of the policymakers and educators who supported what has transmuted into the marginalizing control of programs generated from Title I and NCLB were driven by prejudging based on race. I believe that many honestly had good intentions. However, a question posed rhetorically two decades ago by the distinguished cognitive psychologist Asa Hilliard (and responded to with silence from the powers that be) must be asked again: "With all the good intentions and stipulations, why is there still not a systematic practice or pedagogy aimed at developing high intellectual performance in all students instead of instilling marginalizing practices for students of color, especially those in urban areas?" (Hilliard, 1991/

1995). The type of pedagogy that is needed, which Dr. Hilliard inspired me to develop, is the Pedagogy of Confidence: the artful use of the science of learning to generate High Operational Practices that empower and support students and teachers to fearlessly pursue demonstrations of high intellectual performance that can lead to self-directed learning and self-actualization.

The Pedagogy of Confidence, like the gifted-type education it reflects, could be an advantageous systematic practice, but such pedagogy has not yet been sanctioned as a systematic response for underachieving school-dependent students. The reason is most eloquently captured in the words of Albert Einstein: "No problem can be solved from the same level of consciousness that created it."

The Devaluing Repercussions of Control

One of the dominant consequences of the fixation on control in urban education has been that the system continues to be one of the only institutions in our society that devalues its clients (i.e., the students). Their input is rarely sought to better reflect their strengths or interests or needs, which would ensure more relevant service through the practices used with them or the programs designed for them. Most of us would have to admit that education for these students has assumed the form of subjugated attendance rather than participation in a learning community (Lafley & Charan, 2008). The level of consciousness that has fueled the control policies not only disregards the irrefutable neuroscience findings about the brain and its vast capacity for intellectual development, but has also produced mandated assessments and programmatic practices that have been constructed in a way that totally ignores the realities of the students they are supposed to address (Hilliard, 1995; Sternberg, 1998/2006).

Static, limiting assessment. Uncritical application of standardized assessment ignores student potential and diversity. The focus on the "achievement gap" to compare the distance in scores on standardized tests between races and ethnic groups has navigated us away from the real purpose of assessment: measuring individual learning growth and what affects it (Hilliard, 1991/1995). This is compounded by the fact that standardized achievement tests focus neither on intellectual development nor on the dynamic feature of learning potential. Reading and math skills are only approximations of learning (Hess & Henig, 2008), and thus the vast range of intellectual capacity of school-dependent students is not assessed. This makes another truth abundantly clear: Characterizing standardized tests as a means to assess learning potential or diagnose the causes of learning problems is invalid (Feuerstein, 1978; Sternberg, 1998).

The concomitant invalidating reality about standardized tests for assessing school-dependent students is that the tests are not constructed in a manner that is reflective of the diversity of the students. Robert Sternberg (1998, p. 199) explains it more directly, illustrating the reasons for misperceptions in assessing our school-dependent students of color: In measuring intelligence we must take into account people, tasks, and situations, not only in cross-cultural or multicultural measurement, but also in all measurement. The conventional method has been that one constructs a test of intelligence, and then if one wishes to use it in new ways, one adapts it, with such adaptations being remarkably superficial. For example, a test of intelligence will simply be translated, or at best, some of the informational content (if it is a test of crystallized abilities) will be modified to suit the culture (e.g., values of a group, locale, and profession) to which the test is to be given. But this kind of modification is largely cosmetic.

This superficial, cosmetic modification of assessments ignores the effects of culture on language and cognition, despite widespread acknowledgment that culture molds language. These types of modifications fail to take into account that language represents a way of thinking. We know that virtually all tests, irrespective of type, rely on language or communicative behavior. Yet overlooked is the fact that most of the students in poor, urban districts are African American and have their own cultural linguistic form (language or dialect). It has been well documented that incongruence between the communicative behavior or language of the test giver (or constructor) and that of the students can result in bias. Tester misinterpretation, misunderstanding, or rejection of the test taker's responses can lead to faulty assessments of cognitive, social, and language behavior, resulting in students being labeled as language disordered, learning disabled, or in extreme cases, emotionally disturbed (Delpit, 1995; Taylor & Latham-Lee, 1991, pp. 37–43). Samuda added a historical perspective on the inappropriateness of standardized tests that have not been normed on the group being tested, pointing out that any group identified as "minority" has always scored lower on standardized tests regardless of the race or ethnicity of the group: the Irish of the 1900s, the southern and eastern Europeans of the 1910s and '20s, and the Blacks and Spanish-speaking groups of the mid-20th century (Samuda, 1998, p. 3).

Sternberg (1998, p. 198) also points out another disregarded reality that cannot be denied: Prejudicing misinterpretations have not been confined to formal assessment. Disconnections and misjudgments that teachers are led to make about the potential of culturally different students are also affected by conceptions of intelligence and language differences. Conceptions affect teachers' evaluations of their students' performance. So many of us have experienced that these conceptions among teachers can vary so greatly that within a single school students can perform with different success with different teachers in part as a function of match versus mismatch of what was considered by teachers to be intelligent behavior.

The conceptions teachers have about the linguistic differences of their students are extremely problematic. Teachers with whom I have worked across the country have shared with me what Dewey found so many years ago: They do not know how to move their students from the linguistic form that has been practical and social for them to the standard form on which they are assessed or from which they must construct meaning (Dewey, 1933). Without training regarding linguistic differences, teachers often consider students' linguistic form inferior and generalize this to signify inferior thinking. Cunningham's research (cited in Delpit, 1995) shows that when teachers assess comprehension by using miscue analysis, they are more likely to correct reading miscues that are dialect related than those that are not. This perception of inferiority is sometimes communicated directly to the students, who understandably are sensitive to how their primary language is regarded. To demean their language is to demean their culture and identity.

Disenfranchising instruction. The limited consciousness that drives control policies has also had devastating effects in classrooms, turning instruction into the antithesis of the Pedagogy of Confidence. I have witnessed instruction in hundreds of classrooms more reflective of Friere's (1970) *Pedagogy of the Oppressed*: (a) controlled instructional guidelines causing a downward shift to extended literacy blocks, where teaching is restricted to basal series; (b) controlled pacing guides with alignment neither to the students' strengths or interests, nor to the actual assessments that were supposed to determine their needs; (c) eradication of exposure to the arts or to information outside basal readers or outdated texts that could expand students' frame of reference, thus curtailing their ability to infer meaning about topics that remain foreign to them; and (d) exclusion of enrichment options or credentialing courses that could increase opportunities for students. The additional heinous reality is that lessons taught that reflect the instructional guidelines or pacing guides rarely focus on the cognitive skills required by the standards (e.g., evaluation, analysis, problem solving), thus inhibiting students from meeting these standards and decreasing their rate of learning.

Inhibiting structures. The decreased rate of learning caused by static, limiting assessment and disenfranchising instruction perpetuates segregated academic tracking and holding students back, placing thousands of students on a repressed or even downward trajectory. Teachers have also reported that disproportionate numbers of students of color are being relegated to and trapped in dead-end special education categories because such programs are perceived as the only resource available for helping students who are not succeeding. I find it more accurate to describe these students as those for whom traditional education, which does not reflect them, has failed. The lack of achievement that results from traditional practices, concomitant with the pressure of control policies, has led to another form of "assessment practices" that seem destined only to oppress—rather than uplift—the very students in need of extra support. Many states that try to avoid sanctions derived from test-driven accountability "push-out" low-achieving students to try to raise test scores. Because "subgroups" are identified for district accountability measures, students labeled as "minorities in designated subgroups" are more likely to be pushed out, leaving them in a neglected limbo (Orfield, Losen, Wald, & Swanson, 2004).

The Disavowed Paradigm:
Teacher Perceptions Versus Student Beliefs

I have witnessed the oppressive effects that stigmatizing practices have had on both teachers and their students in schools across the country, and there is no wonder why: People shape themselves to fit their world (Piaget, 1950; Whyte, 2002). The world that teachers and students share is their school—a world where the consequences arising from stigmatizing sanctions and practices reverberate in a negative synergy that produces antipathetic reciprocal relationships that leave both students and teachers demotivated. These oppressive effects also foster conditions in schools that are oppositional to the hierarchy of needs identified by Maslow (1943): survival needs, physical safety, social connections and belonging, self-esteem, and self-actualization. Sanctions have left principals and teachers feeling insecure in their abilities and unsafe in their professional lives. The learning growth of their students—which has been minimized, stalled, or atrophied because of the stigmatizing practices—has left the educators feeling ill-equipped to restore motivation or revive the speed of learning of which the students are capable. This feeling of incompetence among the teachers extinguishes their confidence and smothers their passion. They become weary. Feelings of repression mount and are passed along from teachers to their students (Alpert, 1976; Friere, 1970). Teachers react to the oppressive conditions by withdrawing from socializing in school or collaborative instructional planning, viewing these activities as fruitless. Students respond to the negative atmosphere with significant resistant behaviors (shutting down or acting out). They feel the apprehension of their teachers and translate this as the teachers not caring or not believing in their capacity to learn. The teachers often misinterpret the students' behavior as showing a lack of caring. Both sets of perceptions are too often very far from the truth, but the fear and apprehension exacerbated by the sanctions and perpetual focus on weakness have fueled antagonistic survival techniques from administrators, teachers, and their students that reinforce debilitating learning conditions— producing more suffering for all. Together the students and the educators live lives of quiet desperation, where the complexity of school life requires an enormous reservoir of energy that is never replenished. Instead of waking into a day in which there is a possibility of grace, of being "gifted," of being surprised, they wake into a day in which they feel as if they cannot possibly complete everything, cannot possibly measure up (Whyte, 2002, CD 4).

The reality of these debilitating conditions has been confirmed in schools around the United States through the Instructional Assessment conducted in the first stage of a partnership between a school district and NUA. Teachers report that at the core of the debilitating conditions are the same stressors identified by Costa and Garmston (2001, 2007): lack of power and efficacy; reduction of teaching to a mandated rubric or a set of steps and competencies; feelings of isolation; and skepticism produced when data regarding student achievement are used for political, evaluative, or coercive purposes. The stress they feel has blinded them to the point that they feel they have lost sight of their moral compass. The ideals and values that propelled them and countless others into teaching (e.g., the sense of mission, solidarity with and empathy for students, the courage to challenge mainstream knowledge and conventional wisdom, improvisation, and passion for social justice) have been beaten down so much that they no longer feel the motivational imperative that directed their attention and made them feel self-actualized (Nieto, 2009). They despairingly sense a loss of their creativity from prolonged use of scripted programs and narrow guidelines, leaving them to feel fear, apathy, and disengagement.

We have learned from neuroscience that the stress teachers feel causes suffering not only on the emotional level but on the cognitive and physical levels as well. Under stress the body releases the hormone cortisol, which impairs cognitive functions such as creativity and comprehension while also reducing blood flow in the top frontal lobes of the brain, which are responsible for "on your feet thinking" (Jensen, 1998). The result is "sick schools" where the prevailing culture of malaise short-circuits the ability to confidently make decisions about the pedagogy needed to nurture effective engagement. We have observed caring, well-meaning teachers and their principals going through the motions to function while in a blinding state of disequilibrium. The stress enveloping the school is so profound that they do not even recognize the misalignment between their good intentions to engage students and the instructional methods they use. Their ability to provide the enriching pedagogy their students desperately need to mobilize and accelerate learning for the achievement on which they will all be judged is profoundly impaired. In other words, students of teachers who are bombarded by such stressors are denied the animation and clarity of direction needed to motivate them.

The reciprocal nature of relationships causes the stress of teachers to inflict upon students the same kinds of debilitating effects the teachers themselves experience. The too-often ignored, drastic difference is that for many school-dependent students, school is their only refuge for escaping the stress of their daily lives; for many it is their only hope for enrichment to stimulate dreams of the possibilities the world might hold for them. The debilitating, unavoidably reciprocal relationship between stressed, unsupported teachers and the students in their charge is particularly toxic for adolescents. Pedro Noguera (2008) notes that adolescence can no longer be defined as a period coinciding with middle school; instead, it is the physiological period of puberty, which is now starting earlier and lasting into the twenties (Sylwester, 2007). This is the time when the inextricable interrelationship between emotion and cognitive development is most affected. This is the period when passion and relationships animate the core of students' existence. They are the beacons that attract students' attention and stimulate inquiry and exploration. The emotions feed the inherent cognitive cravings for *engagement* (stimulated through relationships, voice, choice, and purpose), *challenge* (aroused through hypothetical thinking, analogous thinking, syllogistic thinking, and philosophical thinking), and *feedback* (which guides reflection, metacognition, evaluation, and cause-and-effect thinking). Adolescence is a period when students are sophisticated enough to want to interpret the cause for their teachers' weariness and lack of passion. The student surveys conducted as part of the NUA Instructional Assessment indicate that considerable percentages of students interpret this weariness as teachers not caring or not believing in their capacity to learn. This belief is compounded by the marginalizing language they hear being used to describe them (i.e., minority, low achiever, disadvantaged, special education). They recognize this as the positional language that it is: power *over* rather than power *with* (Delpit, 1995; Hilliard, 1991/1995; Mahiri, 1998). They respond to this toxic reality first by skepticism, pushing back to test the reality in which they find themselves. This skepticism is often followed by other resistant behaviors or emotions, such as aliteracy (unwillingness rather than inability to learn) and apathy, resulting in 7,000 students dropping out daily and millions more never realizing their potential, believing that the limited trajectory they experience is the best they are capable of achieving.

But there are millions of students who tenaciously stay in school. It is undeniable that some of the students with lives challenged by poverty stay in school because they rely on school as their home away from home—the place they seek to feel safe. And millions of others stay because they secretly hold on to the memory of the promise made to them as they enthusiastically looked forward to kindergarten: School would be the place where they would learn and would be guided on the path to a liberating future. However, these students are among the first to recognize that there is an enormous gap between their performance, their potential, and what they are provided with in school. They recognize the gap between those students who are valued and engaged and those who are less valued and disengaged (National Urban Alliance, 2010). They are savvy enough to know that those in power in the schools say that they want them to be self-directed learners, but then sentence them to a "separate reality" void of the enrichment, venues, or strategies that inspire or guide self-directed learning, restricting them from self-actualization. These students intuitively recognize that they have been rendered invisible, becoming data sets or pawns in a system where their lives are narrated for them by those control policies and assessment practices that reinforce a "fixed mindset" (Dweck, 2000) about their intellectual capabilities.

The persistent ideology used to narrate the lives of school-dependent students, which has been surmised through data mining of their scores as if they are invisible, has steered us to disregard many realities. We disregard the reality that the data that have been translated as weaknesses represent human beings with aspirations and needs that have been affected by debilitating circumstances outside and inside of school. We disregard the learning growth that happens in spite of the reality of the challenging conditions many battle outside of school. We disregard the stigmatizing practices that make these students feel they do not belong. We disregard the fact that the blatant, restrictive focus on their weakness strips them of their self-esteem or of their dreams of possibilities that would motivate them. We disregard the search for their strengths. And we disregard everything capable of amplifying their intellectual development or affecting their motivation for self-directed learning and self-actualization. The disregard for all of these realities constitutes an egregious sin of omission in urban education. This omission has derailed us from identifying the practices that could generate motivation and mitigate debilitating realities outside of school, which was in fact the original purpose of the Title I funding for which so many fought. This omission has incited many to buy into a Machiavellian framework: When you begin with low expectations, even the slightest growth produced by marginalizing practices can be touted as exceptional growth for "those other students" incapable of high achievement.

As the control policies behind this sin of omission have evolved, I have watched the humanity of urban students minimized as being superfluous, their engagement insidiously repelled, and their learning tragically halted. We cannot continue to turn a blind eye to what is being done inside of schools to restrict the learning of these students and extinguish their motivation. We must also acknowledge and address the influence on students of their experiences outside of school—experiences that color their frame of reference and impact their learning, and may equip them with higher order intellectual and behavioral "survival" skills that do not fit neatly into preconceived notions of achievement. We have narrated the lives of these students from a perspective distorted by myopic data. We must bring to the surface the truth about the intellectual capacity of school-dependent urban students and what affects its development. And we must shine a light on the powerful Pedagogy of Confidence many unheralded urban teachers have sedulously employed to inspire and fulfill this capacity.

3

Other Disregarded Realities

Obscured Learning Barriers Impacting
African American School-Dependent Students

We claim what we feel we deserve.   —David Whyte

*Are there additional barriers that affect the
intellectual development and learning of
African American school-dependent students?*

INSIDE AND OUTSIDE OF SCHOOL:
DEBILITATING CONDITIONS THAT RESTRICT LEARNING

When we believe in the vast intellectual capacity of all students to achieve at high levels, we are relentless in searching for ways to unleash that capacity. Unfortunately, there are thousands of teachers and principals who deeply believe this capacity resides within their school-dependent students but have expressed to me that their confidence has been shaken by their inability to unleash it. They often feel stymied by students' responses to instruction—resistant behaviors, disengagement, aliteracy—that hold them back from applying this vast capacity so they can realize the potential they possess. This feeling of incompetence is the result of two major oversights in urban education: (a) Students' responses of either resistance or acceptance are at least in part predicated on the specific nature of the pedagogy and curriculum to which they are exposed (Mahiri, 1998, p. 3), and (b) to positively affect the behaviors and learning of school-dependent adolescent students, educators must address what influences those behaviors (Feuerstein, 1978; Feuerstein et al., 2006; Hilliard, 1977; Sylwester, 2007). The grave error of overlooking or neglecting these truths when crafting educational programs for school-dependent students has caused the intellectual capacity of these students to go unrecognized—by teachers and by themselves—and has left the teachers committed to them feeling frustrated and unskilled.

The myopic, underestimating view of the learning ability of under-achieving school-dependent students perpetuates a vicious demotivating cycle of disconnections for them. These disconnects and disregard for their lives happen so often that these students start believing that they do not have the ability to comprehend, and thus they become disengaged. The disengagement is then interpreted as a lack of motivation on the part of the students, which is addressed with punitive responses, which in turn escalate the disengagement, apathy, and stress that inhibit comprehension. These responses are similar to the emotions their teachers experience from the control policies, demoralizing tagging in the school, prescriptive programs, and resulting disengagement of the students.

I remember working as a consultant for several years in a high school in the Cabrini Projects in Chicago. The Cabrini Projects were a housing complex for individuals of low socioeconomic status and were beset with violence. Teachers lamented about the poor attendance and lack of motivation displayed by many of the students there, often never considering the constant stress these students experienced because of the violence that surrounded them. On one occasion I was asked to do a demonstration lesson on similes in an English class where the students were reading the play *Raisin in the Sun* by Lorraine Hansberry. During the briefing session the teacher commented that the students did not seem to be able to "get it" and, as usual, they continued to be generally disinterested and refrained from participation.

I began the lesson by asking the students where the play took place, and not one student knew that the setting was Chicago. No connection to their immediate world had ever been noted for them. This is the same school in which I observed a teacher explaining to his students that the reason he was assigning the next chapter in their textbook was because it would be on the test the next week. One of the students responded to this explanation by saying, "We don't even know if we'll be alive next week." These experiences illuminate two critical reasons for the poor motivation and learning of underachieving school-dependent students: (a) the inattention to connecting to the students' personal frames of reference, which would have assisted them in identifying relevance and building a context for interpreting the play (without which the play became foreign and irrelevant); and (b) a disregard for the experiences these students dealt with on a daily basis that impacted their psyches. In response to uncontrollable violence, the Cabrini Projects were torn down years ago. Yet the area of Chicago in which the Cabrini Projects were previously located is still a region where statistics show an average of one homicide taking place each month (Smith, 2010).

I share these anecdotes to elucidate some of the realities that many school-dependent students face inside and outside of school that influence their motivation. Decontextualized instruction inside school and stress

from the fear they experience outside (and sometime inside) school com-
pound to suppress motivation and diminish learning. I will first examine
the issue of decontextualizing what is taught inside school and the powerful
impact contextualizing can have on unleashing the deep insight, intellectual capacity, and motivation of students who are routinely underestimated
and unengaged.

Decontextualized Instruction

Resistant behaviors of students are very often a reflection of their lack of
confidence in their ability to learn (Comer, 1993; Dweck, 2000; Feuerstein,
1979a). Confidence is knowing what is expected and believing you have
what it takes to meet those expectations. Building such confidence requires
reflective pedagogy in which the teacher is clear about the nature of the task
to be presented, the nature of the type of thinking that will have to be
engaged in to achieve the task, the focus to be explored, and the bridges that
can be made from the focus to the students' frames of reference. In the case
of the class where the demonstration lesson took place, the task was to create similes related to the play *Raisin in the Sun*. To do this, I first had to make
sure the students understood what a simile was: a nonliteral comparison of
two unlike things that uses "like" or "as." To create similes requires many
thinking processes: analysis for determining how the things being compared are alike, reasoning to come to conclusions about the relationship of
the things being compared, and synthesis for combining the comparisons.
I determined that "relationships" was the focus or theme of the play that
would be most engaging and generative for creating comparisons that connected to the students' frames of reference as adolescents. I began the exploration of the theme by using a type of Thinking Map® called a Circle Map.
(Thinking Maps are visual–verbal organizers that assist students in identifying patterns and relationships in their thinking as well as in textual material. A Circle Map is used for defining a concept or theme. The eight types
of Thinking Maps are illustrated in Figure 3.1, and they are detailed more
fully in Chapter 5. Thinking Maps is a registered trademark of Thinking
Maps, Inc. Information about professional development training in Thinking Maps may be found at www.thinkingmaps.com.)

Working with the Circle Map, students gave examples of relationships
and then defined the term "relationships." They were next led through
brainstorming attributes of positive and negative relationships to stimulate
identifying possibilities of things that could be compared to what relationships are like. We discussed the various relationships within the play and
categorized them as positive or negative, but what was most engaging and

FIGURE 3.1 Introducing and Defining Thinking Maps

Thinking Maps and the Frame	Expanded Maps

The Circle Map is used for seeking context. This tool enables students to generate relevant information about a topic as represented in the center of the circle. This map is often used for brainstorming.

The Bubble Map is designed for the process of describing attributes. This map is used to identify character traits (language arts), cultural traits (social studies), properties (sciences), or attributes (mathematics).

The Double Bubble Map is used for comparing and contrasting two things, such as characters in a story, two historical figures, or two social systems. It is also used for prioritizing which information is most important within a comparison.

The Tree Map enables students to do both inductive and deductive classification. Students learn to create general concepts, (main) ideas, or categories headings at the top of the tree, and supporting ideas and specific details in the branches below.

The Brace Map is used for identifying the part–whole, physical relationship of an object. By representing whole–part and part–subpart relationships, this map supports students' spatial reasoning and understanding of how to determine physical boundaries.

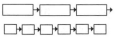

The Flow Map is based on the use of flowcharts. It is used by students for showing sequences, order, timelines, cycles, actions, steps, and directions. This map also focuses students on seeing the relationships between stages and substages of events.

The Multi-Flow Map is a tool for seeking causes of events and the effects. The map expands when showing historical causes and for predicting future events and outcomes. In its most complex form, it expands to show the interrelationships of feedback effects in a dynamic system.

The Bridge Map provides a visual pathway for creating and interpreting analogies. This map is used for understanding and applying analogical reasoning and metaphorical concepts for deeper content learning.

The Frame
The "Metacognitive" Frame is not one of the eight Thinking Maps. It may be drawn around any of the maps at any time as a "meta-tool" for identifying and sharing one's frame of reference for the information found within one of the Thinking Maps. These frames include personal histories, culture, belief systems, and influences such as peer groups and the media.

illustrative of their frame of reference as adolescents and their vast experiences of both types of relationships was their deep insight about what makes a relationship positive or negative. These discussions and the identification of attributes of positive and negative relationships provided the context needed for creating the similes, opening up a plethora of possibilities. These are examples of the similes the students authored:

- Relationships are like fences. They can keep you together.
- Relationships are like fences. They can pen you in.
- Relationships are like school. You can learn from them.
- Relationships are like the stars, when they are out in the open.
- Relationships are like the seasons. They change.
- Relationships are like the subway, when you have to go underground.
- Relationships can be like the ground. You can get walked on.
- A relationship can be like the trash, when you just throw it away.
- A relationship is like a light switch. You can turn it off and on.
- Relationships can be like glass. You can see right through some.

The facility with which these students were able to create similes illustrates their nimble intellectual capacity. In a 50-minute class period the students were able to disprove not only the negative prejudging about their ability but, equally important, the misrepresentation about their desire to be engaged. I was a total stranger to these students, yet after 30 minutes of priming, the door to their potential and creativity was opened to me.

Fear of Violence

The other reality for these students that must be recognized and revisited when judging them is the impact on their learning of fear arising from violence. Recently a study was done on the impact of violence on test scores in reading, writing, and thinking ability of students living in the very same area of Chicago. It was found that the constant experience of violence actually distorts the brain, causing test scores to deflate dramatically. The reality theorized by this study for students from such areas is haunting: The violent atmosphere created by the monthly homicides that occurred in the area caused students to function at impaired cognitive levels for 1 week out of each month, equaling impaired thinking for 3 months out of the year (Smith, 2010). Given this reality, the fact that the students I had the pleasure to teach for the demonstration lesson could so quickly learn the nature of similes and create similes at such a pace while living in an environment where their cognition was continually assaulted is indicative of two undeniable facts: (a) These students do indeed have vast intellectual capacity, and (b) when such students are provided with pedagogy that aims at explicitly mediating their cognition through scaffolding of skill development and contextualizing by connecting to their frame of reference, cognitive impairments can be mitigated. This demonstration of the intellectual capacity of students when provided with challenging, inviting mediation has been reaffirmed by thousands of believing teachers around the country. Yet, because many of these teachers work in isolation—from the tiny islands of confidence their classrooms provide—vast numbers of students are left to be influenced by the pervasive misperceptions about their intelligence that marginalizing practices have fostered. They are left to claim only what they have been led to believe is the best they can hope for—underachievement and disengagement.

Tethered Self-Perceptions

The misperception underachieving school-dependent students are led to construct about themselves (from either their lived frame of reference, misjudgments about their intelligence, marginalizing language about them, or practices reflective of that language) is played out over and over in urban schools, and it is a reality that is often outside of the consciousness of caring teachers. The students' misperceptions reflect what Carol Dweck calls the "entity theory": the belief that their intelligence is fixed and unchangeable. This theory affects what they believe they are capable and not capable of learning, influencing their self-concept, motivation, goal setting, and tenacity in school (Dweck, 2000).

Self-esteem and self-confidence are concretized during adolescence, when the frontal lobes responsible for self-perception associated with social acceptance, affirmation of strengths, and recognition mature. This is a significant factor for adolescents of color because they are keenly aware of the realities that accompany the stereotypical perceptions attributed to their race or ethnicity. The maturation of their reasoning ability ignites a sophisticated "theory of mind" for them, constructed from the brain's effort to understand the interior motivations for why their teachers perceive them as they do (Medina, 2008, p. 67). These young people are acutely aware of the labels used for them, including designations related to the "achievement gap," and they astutely infer what the labels and designations imply about their intelligence. Theorist Bernard Weiner (1984, 1990) defined this kind of inference as an "attributional inference." Attribution theory addresses how people make sense of their world, particularly how they explain the things they observe and experience. The attributions students make for their successes and failures determine the impact of those successes and failures (Dweck, 2000, pp. 139–140). For adolescents, attributions are seminal to their self-concept and how they relate to those whose actions they infer reflect negative or pejorative opinions about them.

How adolescents' theory of mind develops (what Piaget describes as moving from egocentric perspectives to being able to decenter and see through another's perspective) is very much affected both by their experiences outside school as well as by the beliefs, practices, and structures they are subjected to inside school. But we have new hope regarding the negative impact debilitating challenges have on learning. The study on the impact of violence on learning cited earlier (Smith, 2010) illustrated that with the right support, the dysfunctions caused by exposure to violence can be mitigated. If we are to truly commit to reversing underachievement, we need to begin by appreciating the power students' frames of reference have on their learning. Then we can work to design pedagogy that can eclipse the negative effects of the debilitating conditions they experience and optimize the potential of the strengths and resiliency they so clearly possess.

THE IMPACT OF RACE AND CULTURE ON
COGNITION AND ACHIEVEMENT

The majority of urban school-dependent students are students of color, particularly students of African ancestry. This ancestry, and the legacy of the prejudice associated with it, is undeniably pivotal in molding the frame of reference through which they see themselves and how they believe others see them. It is obvious that perceptions affect the self-concept needed for motivation, self-directed learning, and self-actualization. Addressing the impact race and culture have on thinking and learning is challenging for even the most skilled and well-meaning educators. I have witnessed the difficulty many fine teachers have discussing culture and race because of the legacy of race in the United States. As a result of this difficulty, recognition of the impact culture and race have on learning is minimized, ignored, or fearfully neglected. However, I have found that when teachers have the benefit of experiencing safe environments that enable them to engage in discussions (although still often uncomfortable ones) in which they can explore culture and how cultural references (values, traditions, rituals) influence who we are, their frames of reference often broaden to recognize the influence race and stereotypes can have on learning. These teachers expand their pedagogical considerations for the language they use, how they assess how their students infer meaning from what they are introduced to, and the instructional choices they make for priming their students—they become more sensitive to how they contextualize learning for the students. These considerations are of paramount importance for creating the trusting relationships needed to increase students' motivation and learning.

Cultural Frame of Reference and Learning

Because race and culture are topics that are difficult to approach, I have found that an entry point for the conversation is an initial exploration of culture in general. Then the discussion can move on to defining what we associate with our own culture (what has influenced who we are) and lastly reflecting on how our own culture impacts what we do and why we see the world as we do. These reflections help us recognize that we all have a cultural frame of reference through which we perceive the world, and it affects how we respond to all the experiences we encounter. When we understand the impact our cultural frame of reference has on our own behavior, we better appreciate and can respond to the influence our students' frames of reference have on their learning and their motivation.

Culture and Motivation

The term "culture" has two defining aspects. In a general sense, culture as it pertains to all humankind is said to develop as a result of social experience, education, and discipline (Meyers, 1966). In this respect, all individuals in a particular society develop a cultural character. The other aspect of culture is recognized as "a purposive system of behavior norms, values, and attitudes which its members follow by force of habit" (Wilson, 1978, p. 162). In this second respect, three understandings are important to shedding light on how our culture influences us:

- The experiences of the cultural group we affiliate with affect how we respond to (assimilate and accommodate ourselves to) a particular situation. In other words, our cultural group affects our behavior patterns.
- Experiences within our culture influence our personal goals, values, and attitudes.
- One's cultural frame of reference is a filtering agent. Cultural myths and legends affect how we translate history, and that translation affects how we view our relationship to the world. (Wilson, 1978)

Recognition of these aspects of culture confirm why we cannot ignore the frames of reference of African American students and the perceptions these frames create, which are colored by the racial identity of the individuals. This identity is cast from the reality, shared through their families and the history they study, that their ancestors were brought to this country against their will, as an enslaved people exposed to heavily systematized hostility (Cobbs & Grier, 1977). The history of the hostility, shared explicitly or implicitly, reminds them that their enslaved ancestors developed "survival techniques" in order to preserve their lives. These techniques included passivity and suppression of any demonstration of exceptional ability for fear of being recognized as a threat. They are reminded of how the survival techniques continued to be practiced by many African Americans when slavery was abolished. Even when discrimination was declared unconstitutional, doors to white institutions only gradually (and often begrudgingly) opened to African Americans, and prejudice continued to prevail. This was felt even within the confines of the African American communities themselves. The students are reminded that schools in those communities were denied appropriate funding, and the quality of education suffered (*Brown v. Board of Education*). They hear through family legends that it was considered a feat if African American students succeeded in institutions of higher learning, and yet even that success was responded to by denial of the economic or social benefits such achievement should have availed them. Ancestral sagas often include the reality that many who did succeed were alienated from their roots, with no substitution available. Black scholars entered from the outside, and their contributions were those of outsiders (Cobbs & Grier, 1977, p. 29).

As educators, we must first recognize how our own culture influences how we see and respond to the world. This recognition, then, will make more comprehensible how the legacy of enslavement and residual institutional racism (which in many places have continued into the present) have been incorporated into the cultural frame of reference of our African American students. These factors affect them emotionally, and their cognition and resultant learning are in turn impacted.

The existence of these historical issues has prompted much experimental and empirical research over the years. Unfortunately, the research is rarely used to inform understandings of the how these realities affect the behaviors, needs, and strengths of African American students, so the realities and their effects remain obscured and ignored. Some of the effects of the obscured realities on these students include:

- *Inhibitions caused by inferiority complexes:* These inhibitions curb a wide range of assertive competitive acts, most of which are healthy for confidence building, goal setting, and self-actualization (Delpit, 1995; Mahiri, 1998; Noguera, 2003; Steele & Aronson, 2004; Torrance, 1977).

- *Sociocultural deprivation:* Feuerstein described this phenomenon as a lack of connecting new experiences to one's cultural references, which then affects cognitive functioning by short-circuiting cultural anchors needed for expanding confidence, intellectual capabilities, and motivation (Feuerstein, 1979a; Noguera, 2003).

- *Absence of motivation:* This lack of motivation results from a deficit of encouragement, either directly—through marginalizing programs and terms, misguided teacher perceptions of students' ability, or the lack of parental pressure—or indirectly—through the lack of access to role models or exposure to opportunities or careers that would demonstrate the "payoff" of education as a catalyst for seeking success in school (Averch, Carroll, Donaldson, Kiesling, & Pincus, 1975). Often when these students are motivated, the motivation is expressed in behaviors that are looked upon and labeled as unsophisticated, stubborn, disruptive, or negative. It should be duly noted, however, that because these same characteristics are also found in many of the most effective, productive, and creative people, labels for these behaviors are recast as positive traits when they appear on checklists of characteristics for gifted programs (Delpit, 1995; Dweck, 2000; Mahiri, 1998; Torrance, 1977).

- *Perceiving a stereotype threat, or fear of being at risk of confirming a negative stereotype about one's group:* Such perceptions can lead students to engage in self-handicapping strategies such as reducing practice time for a task, and they can produce a diminished sense of belonging to the stereotyped group. Consistent perception of a stereotype threat in school can reduce the degree to which school is valued (Steele & Aronson, 2004).

NEUROBIOLOGY AND SCHOOL-DEPENDENT STUDENTS

The Impact of Race on Neurobiology and Learning

Most of the research described above is not new. Much is work I reviewed 30 years ago for my doctoral studies. Sadly, in spite of the existence of the research—which has been revalidated—it still is not used to inform curriculum writing or the design of programs created for underachieving school-dependent students of African American descent. In fact, I find that when I share this research in professional development sessions in the urban districts with which my organization partners, most teachers are not even aware of its existence. More recently, the field of neuroscience has proffered research that unequivocally confirms the impact that the realities African

American students experience have on their learning. Research in neuroscience demonstrates that stress associated with prejudice, degradation, stereotype threat, reaction to abuse, feelings of failure, inability to succeed, positional or marginalizing language, and feelings of low self-esteem not only causes production of cortisol—which inhibits comprehension, resulting in low achievement—but stress can also rewire the brain to cognitively predispose an individual to keep doing the same things over and over. This repetition includes patterns of poor performance as well as self-sabotaging behaviors. The reason for this is that stress causes regions of the brain associated with executive decision making and goal-directed behaviors to shrivel, whereas, at the same time, brain sectors linked to habit formation bloom. As a consequence, goal-oriented behaviors decline and negative habits perpetuate and flourish. Even perceived threats or memories of threats can cause constant hyperactivation of the stress response, further enhancing repeated negative patterns (Angier, 2009). The negative repercussions of stress are compounded for school-dependent students when they are confined to prescribed remedial programs that supersede the enrichment needed to stimulate interests and develop strengths. Stress is exacerbated if there is no outlet for frustration, no sense of control, no social support, or no impression that something better will follow (Sapolsky, 2003, p. 88). In other words, the cultivated schooling reality for these students intensifies stress, thus fueling underachievement.

It is critical also to consider several other impairing effects of stress on learning and achievement so that practices and structures can be sought to mitigate these effects and stem the tide of underachievement. These effects include impediment of creativity, explicit memory, and the ability to sort relevant from irrelevant information (Jensen, 1998); barriers that disable input from reaching those parts of the brain responsible for language acquisition, restricting how meaning is constructed (Delpit, 1995); reduction of blood flow in the top frontal lobe area that activates on-your-feet thinking (Jensen, 1998); and the impairment of immune function (*ScienceDaily*, 2009).

Recognizing the deep effects race and the cultural frame of reference have on belief, behaviors, and learning of school-dependent African American students is the first step to ameliorating how these students are actually perceived and subsequently how they feel they are perceived, critical considerations in transforming urban education.

Poverty and Learning

As with stress, the impact of another factor detrimental to the learning of school-dependent students has been ignored for far too long—the effect of poverty on learning. It has been acknowledged through Title I that poverty limits the exposure and enrichment needed for academic success, but there are many other debilitating repercussions of poverty that can no longer be ignored. Addressing these repercussions can enable development of intellectual capacities and the identification of support services and practices that could mitigate the preponderance of underachievement that is sustained in urban districts (Comer, 1993; Feuerstein, 1980).

I will begin by reviewing the effects of the lack of exposure caused by poverty. By the age of 3, the exposure middle-income children experience has increased their working vocabulary to two times the size of the vocabulary of low-income children (Toppo, 2008). This puts school-dependent students at a deficit from the very beginning of their school experience, which is a critical problem when students in many states are assessed and tracked based on their vocabulary before entering kindergarten. Without explicit accelerated methods of language development—which tracking restricts—this problem increases with the onslaught of technical or esoteric language inherent in discipline-related texts (Cooper, 2009). The exposure and discussion around the exposure are what Feuerstein calls "mediation": purposefully selected cognitive stimuli, training, or enrichment needed for learning and academic achievement (Feuerstein, 1979; Feuerstein, Feuerstein, & Falik, 2010). (Mediation is described at length in Chapter 4.) Gladwell (2008) has more recently described the effects of such mediation on the success of exceptional achievers in his book *Outliers*. Both sets of research have been substantiated by neuroscience studies that demonstrate that such mediation induces the development of neural patterns that make the learning process more efficient and therefore more expansive (Feuerstein, 1979a; Holloway, 2003; Jensen, 1998; Lareau, 2003; Medina, 2008).

Poverty also causes physiological impairments that have a major affect on underachievement yet go unaddressed. What would seem to be the most obvious impairment needing attention is poor eyesight. Poverty keeps students from receiving the full eye examinations needed to identify the spectrum of visual impairments. The shocking reality is that certain behaviors associated with poor eyesight have recently been shown to be misdiagnosed as attention deficit disorder (Fisher, 1998). The absence of adequate eye exams leaves undetected disorders that inhibit learning—disorders that could easily be remedied for innumerable numbers of students living in poverty (Johnson, 2007).

Another effect of poverty that should seem obvious is malnutrition. Food programs in schools have been created to address this problem, but severe poverty relegates students to being without adequate food in the evenings and on weekends, leaving scores of them malnourished. Malnutrition creates lesions in the prefrontal cortex of the brain, impairing higher order thinking and problem solving. Malnutrition also impairs the development of neural systems, resulting in stunted development of language and executive cognitive functions such as paying attention, remembering details, and planning. Neuroscience now illustrates that the debilitating effects of the lesions can be mitigated with appropriate cognitive mediation in higher level thinking tasks (Toppo, 2008).

In addition, perhaps the most insidious effect of poverty is the lead poisoning to which numerous students living in low-income housing have been exposed. The danger of lead poisoning has garnered national attention, but considerations of the impact of this poison on learning are rarely discussed when identifying learning disabilities of students. Long-term exposure to lead affects cognitive and neurobiological functioning, producing outcomes such as diminished intellectual functioning, decreased proficiency in basic academic skills, increased delinquency, and increased risk for antisocial behaviors in adolescents (Lidsky & Schneider, 2005). Fortunately, these side effects, too, can be mitigated with appropriate cognitive mediation.

UNDERSTANDING THE CAUSES for the behaviors of our school-dependent students should enable us to expand our thinking about how to address these causes as well as the prejudices that are promulgated about these students. Acknowledging how race and poverty affect the self-perceptions of adolescents of color makes it clear that any individual (regardless of race or ethnicity) confronted with the same types of experiences would have their emotions destabilized, and their learning would suffer enormously. When we recognize the realities of the experiences of these students inside and outside of school, the consideration should not be why these students fail to achieve, but rather, how so many learn in spite of the debilitating conditions they are relegated to endure.

But they do learn. Not only do they learn, these students are propelled by the same human imperative that drives us all. They yearn to be self-actualized. However, as Maslow (1943) postulated so definitively, self-actualization cannot happen when the other needs in the hierarchy lay on the precipice. If acknowledgment of the impact of the realities of these students' lives and the inner drive they harbor (which becomes muted by control policies that fuel marginalizing beliefs, practices, and structures) can be channeled to change theories about the potential of these students, we can generate new energy and commitment for the pursuit of pedagogical practices that can serve as antidotes to the factors that impede their learning and demotivate them. The recurring question asked decades ago by Ron Edmonds, and more recently by Pedro Noguera, reverberates once again: Do we have the will to move on this acknowledgment (Edmonds, 1979; Noguera, 2003)? We cannot change the out-of-school conditions, but we can consider the way we judge, penalize, and design practices and structures to respond to the behaviors and achievements of these students. We ardently *need to believe* in their intellectual capacity as well as have confidence in our own ability to inspire that capacity.

PART II

The Practices

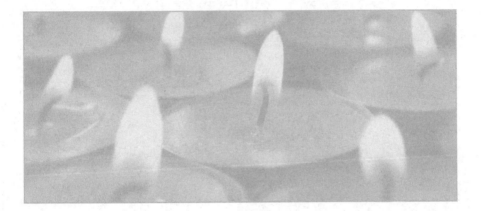

When you change the way you look at things,
the things you look at change.

—Wayne Dyer

4

Divining Intelligence

The Transformative Theory and Practice
of Reuven Feuerstein

*Human beings have the unique characteristic of being able to
modify themselves no matter how they start out. Even inborn
barriers and traumas can be overcome with belief and the right
mediation.* —Reuven Feuerstein

*What is the premier research underlying the
Pedagogy of Confidence?*

I don't remember exactly when I first learned about the bell curve, but I
know that it wasn't during my undergraduate studies, because the open
classroom education I was studying was built on a philosophy that espoused
facilitating learning growth for all students, so we didn't look at theory that
distinguished students. It wasn't until sometime during coursework related
to general educational administration, as well as the identification procedures for gifted programs, that I encountered the theory that used a statistical scalpel to amputate half the student population from projections of
high intellectual performance and actualizing possibilities for their future.
The restrictiveness of the bell curve ideology compelled me to aim the Pedagogy of Confidence at much more than reversing the underachievement of
those who fell at the lower end of the curve. The Pedagogy of Confidence
aims at "divining" for the vast intellectual capacities and strengths that are
innate to school-dependent students so they can be amplified and optimized for self-directed learning and self-actualization.

I use the metaphor of divining because when you divine for a needed
resource, there is a belief in and the recognition of the preciousness of that
resource. When you believe in the intellectual capacity of school-dependent
students, you do not see yourself as a teacher alone. You see yourself as a
seeker divining for the much-needed valuable potential that lies underneath
the surface. "Initially, as a diviner, you are only the bystander, but slowly as
you pay more attention you find the part of you that has the ability: the

ability to put your hands on the expectant outer wrists and make the hazel wand stir . . . make the mind stir" (Whyte, 2002, CD 5).

Almost all of the students I have taught have confirmed the philosophy that I adopted 30 years ago: Providing practices proffered in gifted education could reverse underachievement. However, within my classes there were students for whom my techniques did not seem to work. I recognized the critical impact culture and poverty had on learning (i.e., culture creating learning patterns antithetical to traditional teaching practices, and poverty rendering students devoid of requisite experiences and nourishment needed to build the skills required for traditional academic achievement). I theorized that for these underperforming students, and for the many like them throughout the schools, the impact of traditional methods was so limited that their cognition underfunctioned, causing impairment of their academic learning ability. These impairments were (and continued to be) interpreted and labeled as learning disabilities. This label, in turn, caused these students to be generalized as being "unable" to learn to an average level. They represented the lower end of the bell curve (someone had to) and therefore were assumed to be incapable of ever leaving that position.

Like so many other teachers committed to divining for the intelligence of these students, I set out on a quest for an assessment tool that would be capable of literally diagnosing and addressing the cause of cognitive impairments, which traditional assessment was incapable of doing. I sought a tool that was in fact a divining rod, created specifically to tap the intellectual ability that lies stagnant due to a lack of experiences that stimulate academic learning. I knew that a tool with such power would not only confirm the belief of teachers in the vast intellectual capacity of their underachieving students, it would also reinvigorate teachers' confidence in their ability to activate the intellectual capacity of their students whose achievement was impaired. This tool would motivate teachers to search for practices that elicited this capacity in their students, allowing them to reverse the seemingly eternal relegation to the lower end of the bell curve. My unwavering quest led me to the transformational, seemingly miraculous work of Dr. Reuven Feuerstein.

I discovered Feuerstein in an educational journal article that described how after the Holocaust he had committed himself to work to identify the potential of displaced Jewish children—children who had lost their parents or who had been subjected to concentration camps that imprisoned their bodies and stunted the growth of their intelligence (Hobbs, 1980). Prompted by belief in the vast intellectual capacity of all people, Feuerstein was determined to prove that impairments resulting from debilitating conditions—whether environmental, socioeconomic, emotional, cultural, or genetic—were reversible with the right mentally enriching practices. Through his work with these students, he developed his theory of the structural cognitive modifiability of the brain and the transforming effect using specific cognitive strategies for mediating intelligence has on reversing underachievement (Feuerstein, 1980; Feuerstein et al., 2010). His practice involves much more than assessment. It is a comprehensive learning system consisting of three interconnected approaches—Mediation, the Learning Propensity Assessment Device, and Instrumental Enrichment—designed to repair cognitive dysfunctions and accelerate intellectual development. His learning system has been identified as "the most significant innovations in educational psychology of the twentieth century" (Burgess, 2000, p. 149). It profoundly edified my frame of reference, confirmed my belief about intelligence (gleaned from those years I had served as a classroom teacher), and affirmed my understanding about the interconnectedness of culture and learning (derived from my life as a person of color).

SOCIOCULTURAL DEPRIVATION: THE ILLUSIVE INHIBITOR OF INTELLECTUAL DEVELOPMENT

What deepened my commitment to pursue research in Feuerstein's learning system was the way in which he defined sociocultural deprivation and the correlation he made between it and restricted intellectual development. His work with displaced Jewish children led him to realize that an additional circumstance besides the trauma of the Holocaust had greatly impaired their intellectual development. That circumstance was sociocultural deprivation.

Unlike the American definition of sociocultural deprivation, which refers to students not steeped in middle-class Eurocentric culture as being deprived, Feuerstein describes sociocultural deprivation as missing links to one's own culture. He recognized that knowing one's own culture provided the anchor to past history and the adaptation tools needed to strive for the possibilities of one's future. He determined that culture is shared and elaborated through interactions specifically selected by a parent, relative, or teacher (a person he termed a mediator) to expand understanding and develop the intellectual capabilities of a child. These cultural interactions transmit (verbally or through modeling) certain ways of confronting and adapting to new experiences (recognizing one's perceptions of something, gathering needed information, being sensitive to problems, properly defining situations to be responded to, solving problems, and making rational and grounded decisions). When students are disconnected from these cultural interactions, there is a short circuit in the ways of thinking that would enable them to make meaning, interpret, or infer, thus restricting their intellectual development and ability to adapt (Narrol & Giblon, 1984/2001, p. ix).

Feuerstein's students had been deprived of their mediators and of transmission of their culture—and therefore of their ability to effectively adapt to their altered existence. As I read this description of sociocultural deprivation, I was thinking about how this was a reality my students shared: limited intentional transmission of their culture by a parent at home (for a variety of reasons), almost no connection to their cultural heritage in the teaching they received, and glaring absence of their culture in the curriculum. But, I was also thinking about the influence my own bimodal cultural reality had had on me as a child.

When I was young my mother would send my sister and me to spend the summer with our family in Virginia. Often we would make the 11-hour trip by bus, and the ride would involve a transfer in Washington, D.C. It was at this transfer point, the nation's capital, that we experienced the indelible reality of how the world of the South perceived us, because it was there that we would have to move to the back of the bus. For the rest of the journey, all of the rest stops had signs such as "Whites only" or "Negro section," indicating where we could and could not wait or which water fountains and facilities we could and could not use. However, in spite of these searing attempts to make us feel "less than," that we did not belong, I was fortunate to have parents who were constantly telling us about the strength of our family roots and how the legacy of those roots illustrated the potential we had to live up to. Even after my father and mother were divorced and my mother was alone raising three girls, there were only high expectations and affirmations about the possibilities for us in spite of the other defacing realities. I appreciated the restorative effect that knowing my culture had on my considerations of future possibilities and the affirmations I received that motivated me to attain those possibilities. Later in life, I saw the negative impact of sociocultural deprivation on the self-confidence of my students who had been denied a personal cultural orientation.

STRUCTURAL COGNITIVE MODIFIABILITY: THE PHYSIOLOGICAL ASPECTS OF INTELLECTUAL DEVELOPMENT AND LEARNING

Feuerstein assessed the intellectual state of his students by analyzing the thinking processes they employed as they responded to questions and activities he posed through a variety of content, modalities, operations, and abstractions. He observed that when the students were guided through introspective questioning and bridging to familiar experiences, processes indicative of intellectual behavior—such as connecting ideas, classifying them, identifying relationships between them, and hypothesizing about them—were strengthened. This led him to determine that with the appropriate intervention, the structure of the students' thinking processes was ameliorated, or modified, mitigating the negative impact of their debilitating experiences. Such intervention includes introspective questioning that specifically elicits cognitive functions or mental tools that help individuals create meaning in, adapt to, or control their environment, especially comparative behavior, critical analysis, and evaluation. From this determination came Feuerstein's theory of Structural Cognitive Modifiability. The theory elucidates how the structure of one's cognition can be affected by guided interactions (or the lack of guided interactions) that affect the "fundamental processes of thought, learning, and problem solving" (Narrol & Giblon, 1984/2001, p. ix).

Sociocultural deprivation and structural cognitive modifiability both reflect Feuerstein's definition of intelligence: the dynamic process that enables an individual to adapt in response to a need, a novel situation, or changes in the environment. Adaptability involved in intelligence is inherent in both problem solving (which reflects cognitive elements) and creativity (which is kindled by strong motivational elements). In order to adapt, an individual must be equipped with the cognitive tools or functions required to decide upon and differentiate among numerous and almost overwhelming options (Feuerstein et al., 2010, p. 1). Thus, intelligence involves cognition (or ways of thinking or making meaning), which is comprised of cognitive functions that help an individual adapt to or control his or her environment. The structure of these cognitive functions can be changed or modified positively or negatively in response to both external stimuli and internal conditions throughout life—which means that intelligence itself is modifiable.

MEDIATION:
ACCELERATING INTELLECTUAL DEVELOPMENT AND LEARNING

For Feuerstein, intelligence (or adaptability) depends on three different phases of cognitive behavior: (a) taking in information (input phase), (b) reasoning about or thoughtfully operating on information that has been taken in (elaboration phase), and (c) effectively communicating the results of this reasoning (output phase) (Narrol & Giblon, 1984/2001, p. 10). The environment affects the strength of the behaviors in these phases, which is why students who lack certain guided interactions with enriching resources or encounters needed for learning specific types of information develop what Feuerstein identifies as cognitive dysfunctions. While assessing his students, Feuerstein observed that modifying cognitive dysfunctions to optimize intellectual development and learning required assistance in developing the processes that ameliorate the structure of the cognitive functions. Feuerstein found that the most salient catalyst for assisting restructuring of cognitive functions and the development of intelligence was the interaction between the teacher or parent (or mediator) and the student. He used this recognition to codify the type of pedagogical interaction or process that would heighten intellectual capacities to maximize learning. He called this process "mediation" to highlight the notion of interaction between a learner and his or her environment. This interaction is mediated, or transformed, by a mediator who intentionally and specifically aims to make the interaction of the learner with learning experiences more effective. The goal of the mediation process is to elicit from the learner a personal motivation for learning and to provide the strategies needed for efficient and effective learning. The mediator—guided by intention, culture, and emotional investment in his or her learner—organizes and exposes learning experiences to provide the learner with opportunities to deeply investigate information by posing authentic questions strategically framed in the cultural context of the learner. This guided investigation includes probing for elaborations and searching for personal connections, enabling learners to critically analyze tasks and focus on what is relevant to the learning required. The mediator amplifies learning by providing additional examples of concepts being taught and explicit feedback to facilitate acquisition of relevant relationships, expand language development relative to the focus, and fortify both the cognitive skills necessary to master the task at hand as well as those cognitive functions needed throughout life (e.g., focusing on problems or issues, inferring connections, organizing information, sorting relevant from irrelevant information, and classifying information) (Feuerstein, 1980; Feuerstein, Falik, & Feuerstein, 1998; Feuerstein et al., 2010). This dynamic interaction between the mediator and the student is the most important aspect of the mediation process because it allows assessment of understanding and learning to be part of the instructional process (Jackson et al., 1998). These types of quality interactions have been involved in the cultural transmissions parental figures have provided that have accompanied human development and have shaped human experience (developmental and cultural) throughout history. Mediation is not necessarily verbal or language dependent, but it is always intentional; that is, the mediator wants the learner to grasp what is being taught and will do whatever it takes to help the learner do that (Feuerstein et al., 2010, p. 38). The practices that are used in the mediation process are called Mediated Learning Experiences (MLE).

Mediation and cultural transmission in the learning process have often been ignored. However, they are critical factors in accelerating intellectual development and reversing underachievement for school-dependent students. The latest explanation given for stagnant or declining achievement scores in major urban areas around the country makes this alarmingly clear. This argument highlights worsening economic conditions for poor families as a key factor in the reversal of achievement. It is true that poverty inhibits access to enriching resources, but what makes enrichment influential in intellectual development and learning is not simply a resource itself. The direct experience of walking through a museum or seeing a scientist at work does not expand thinking. What expands thinking is the access *plus* the intentional mediation with probing questions and guided discussion that includes purposeful exploration of connections to personal references. These connections then create the mental anchoring that strengthens hypothesizing or theorizing or even philosophizing. Considering that lack of resources or "fatherlessness" is often cited as a possible reason for the reversal of achievement, it is even more critical that schools do what they can to bridge the gap. Thus, access to enrichment accompanied by teachers trained in mediational methods and school staff committed to creating a Mediative Learning Community is now more important than ever. Closing schools and replacing leadership or teaching staff while maintaining instructional methods that lack the mediation more advantaged students receive as pro forma support outside and inside of school typically results only in repetition of unsuccessful results. It is the lack of mediative practices that keeps students dysfunctioning, not the capacity of their brains.

Neuroscience has validated the power of the authentic questioning involved in Feuerstein's mediation process. The research has shown that when a learner makes a decision on the basis of an authentic question, the process engages the executive functions of the prefrontal cortex (Goldberg, 2001). "The executive functions engage a set of skills and capacities that include problem solving, planning, decision making, time management, persistence, risk assessment, judgment, and impulse control" (Miller & Cummings, as cited in Caine & Caine, 2006, pp. 50–52). Mediation enhances a student's ability to adapt to new stimuli so learning can be optimized.

Mediation and Cognitive Deficiencies

Feuerstein has illustrated through the years how most cognitive functions diagnosed as *dys*functional relate to skills measured on standardized tests. He has proven that weaknesses in these cognitive functions that cause learning impairments are directly related to lack of mediation. Feuerstein labeled these weakened cognitive functions as "deficiencies" to bring attention to the type of intervention, modification, or change needed. He contends that the weaknesses seen in school-dependent students are actually deficiencies in the methods by which they process and use particular information rather than structural and elaborative incapacities (Feuerstein, Rand, & Hoffman, 1980; Jensen, 1998). Deficiencies in cognitive functions are most often manifested by the students as attitudinal and motivational deficiencies, poor work habits, or lack of learning sets. Feuerstein (1979b) correlated these deficient cognitive functions to their effects on the three phases of intellectual processing and categorized them as input, process, and output deficiencies.

Input phase. Cognitive function deficiencies that relate to the quantity and quality of data gathered by students as they are confronted by a given problem, object, or experience include:

- Blurred sweeping perception
- Unplanned, impulsive, and unsystematic exploratory behavior
- Impaired receptive verbal tools and concepts
- Impaired spatial and temporal orientation
- Lack of stable systems of spatial and temporal reference
- Lack of or impaired conservation and constancy in the face of transformations in one or more attributes
- Lack of need for precision and accuracy
- Lack of or impaired capacity for relating to two or more sources of information simultaneously

Elaboration phase. Cognitive function deficiencies that relate to factors that impede the efficient use of available data and existing cues include:

- Inadequacies in the definition of a problem
- Inability to select relevant cues
- Lack of spontaneous comparative behavior
- Narrowness of the mental fields
- Lack of or impaired need for summative behavior
- Difficulties in projecting potential relationships
- Lack of need for logical evidence
- Lack of or limited internalization
- Lack of or restricted hypothetical or inferential reasoning
- Lack of or impaired strategies for hypothesis testing
- Lack of planning behavior
- An episodic grasp of reality
- Nonelaboration (nonprocessing) of certain cognitive categories because the necessary labels are not part of the inventory on the receptive level or are not mobilized at the expressive level

Output phase. Cognitive function deficiencies that relate to factors that lead to an inadequate communication of final solutions include:

- Egocentricity
- Blocking
- Lack of or impaired verbal tools for communicating adequately elaborated responses
- Deficiency in visual transport (e.g., completing a given figure on the left side of a page by finding the missing part on the right side and transporting it visually)
- Lack of or impaired need for precision and accuracy in responding
- Trial-and-error responses
- Impulsive acting-out behavior

THE THREE SEPARATE LEVELS were conceived as a means of bringing some order to the array of deficient cognitive functions seen in socioculturally deprived school-dependent students. Interaction does occur among the levels, and Feuerstein felt that awareness of this interaction was of vital significance in understanding the extent and pervasiveness of the factors that impair cognition. Recognition of levels of deficiencies also substantiated the need for a dynamic form of assessment that could identify the root of cognitive deficiencies so that effective mediation strategies could be determined. That is the purpose of the Learning Propensity Assessment Device (Feuerstein, 1979b).

The Learning Propensity Assessment Device: Addressing the Complexities of Assessing Intellectual Development and Learning

Feuerstein's hypothesis that intelligence is a dynamic, constantly changing process led him to the realization that the only way to sufficiently and accurately assess students' thinking and learning potential was through a dynamic process that involved *teaching* them during the assessment process and then analyzing the way in which they applied cognitive functions for *learning*. This became the premise of "dynamic testing"—testing the student in the process of learning (Feuerstein et al., 2010; Narrol & Giblon, 1984, p. 13). This dynamic process (the antithesis of traditional forms of standardized assessment) consists of three distinguishing components: (a) assessment of the fluid processes of thought, perception, learning, and problem solving rather than assessment of the static or unchanging products of prior learning; (b) carefully structured teaching of cognitive principles and processes;

and (c) reassessment of the ways in which the teaching has modified a student in the direction of higher capacity and greater efficiency on similar, albeit different, problems. The triangulating process enabled Feuerstein to determine that cognitive deficiencies are the cause of many learning problems that occur in the various phases of intellectual behavior (input, elaboration, or output phase), allowing an assessor to identify deficiencies in cognitive functions as well as the individual's intellectual capacity for change and growth. Feuerstein formalized this process of dynamic assessment in the Learning Propensity Assessment Device (LPAD), a battery of test–learning–test situations focused on diagnosing the thinking processes themselves by pinpointing cognitive deficiencies, thus allowing the most direct mediation to be prescribed (Feuerstein et al., 1980). Each instrument is constructed with three structural components:

- *A task, problem, or situation* whose mastery requires not only specific problem-solving behaviors, but also grasp of a given principle through application of the relevant cognitive operation
- *An operation:* categorization, seriation, permutation, logical multiplication, analogical or syllogistic reasoning, or any number of others, all of whose appropriate use depends upon prerequisite cognitive functions as well as upon attitudinal and motivational factors
- *A language or modality in which the task is presented:* pictorial, numerical, figural, graphic, verbal, or logicoverbal

The LPAD model is presented graphically in Figure 4.1.

LPAD uncovers and modifies the cognition of the student, as opposed to other assessments, which discover perceived performance deficits that require "remediation." It is aimed at determining the potential of the individual's intellectual behavior to change or be modified. Mediation is the process the assessor uses in LPAD. Mediation operationalizes the theory of structural cognitive modifiability and fosters changes in cognitive functions and learning.

Mediating, observing, and evaluating students' high intellectual performance provides more insight into their potential than standardized tests could ever do (Furth & Wachs, 1974). The more school-dependent students demonstrate performance reflective of high intelligence, the more confident teachers become about reversing the underachievement of these individuals, who have been challenged by barriers that have inhibited them from learning to their full potential (Delpit, 1995; Feuerstein, 1980; Jackson, Lewis, Feuerstein, & Samuda, 1998).

FIGURE 4.1   The LPAD Model

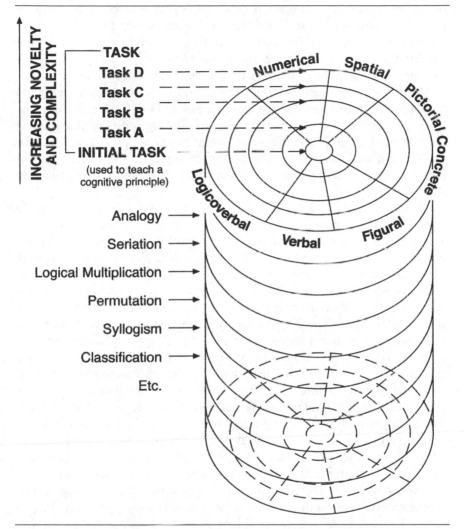

Instrumental Enrichment:
The Programmatic Application of Mediation

Feuerstein knew that maximizing the change shown possible through LPAD would require a cognitive intervention program that could modify identified cognitive dysfunctions as well as elicit students' intellectual potential. Instrumental Enrichment (IE) is that intervention. IE was created with the main goal of increasing the capacity of individuals to become "modifiable" by: (a) exposing them directly to experiences encountered in life, and (b) involving them with formal and informal learning situations. He applied the same theory for IE as for LPAD: Mediation can produce structural cognitive modifiability. The linkage between the LPAD and IE was predicated on various elements in the thinking–learning process that are common to both LPAD tests and IE lesson situations. The common elements (inherent in the mediational process) encompass improvement of deficient cognitive functions; preparation for higher order learning through the establishment of prerequisite functioning; behavioral regulation; development of reflection, insight, and analytical thinking; teaching of cognitive operations and content; provision of performance feedback; and maximization of communication skills.

Feuerstein created a tag line for IE to make obvious his goal for the learner: "Just a minute. Let me think." He created IE to engage the mediation process to develop students' metacognition by providing dialogue between the mediator and the student to enable understanding of learning concepts, explicit cognitive skill training, and practice of the mental operations necessary for independent learning. He purposely designed the program to consist of predominantly figural and symbolic exercises to enable students deficient in specific language to be guided to target and apply cognitive processes without the complication of reading, thus facilitating transfer of the cognitive functions addressed in IE across all disciplines, while at the same time facilitating oral introduction of specific technical and elaborative language to expand vocabulary. The exercises are divided into 14 categories called "instruments," each comprised of tasks aimed at enriching specific cognitive functions such as analytic perception, comparison, classification, temporal relations, and syllogisms. The mediator steers and interprets the thinking processes carried out in the instruments as the tasks become more complex. Using open-ended questions and positive feedback, the mediator assists students in identifying how they are planning to solve problems presented in the various tasks, how they are considering the process to be used for solving the problem, and how they are evaluating what tactics are most successful. In other words, the mediator is making the students conscious of the effectiveness of their thinking to empower them as self-directed learners (Rodriquez & Bellanca, 1996).

Feuerstein has identified the cognitive functions engaged in the IE exercises as the prerequisites for all learning, but especially for self-directed learning and high intellectual performance, focusing on comparative analysis, decision making, problem solving, and achievement. The cognitive functions engaged include:

- Isolation of problems
- Redefinition of problems to ensure accuracy
- Use of systematic search for storing relevant data
- Creation of visual transport (mental images)
- Forecasting (cause/effect)
- Combination of problem solving and then interacting for verification
- Comparative behavior
- Evaluation of relevance versus irrelevance
- Hypothesis testing
- Orientation of things in space
- Proving
- Synthesis of data
- Analytic perception
- Labeling (Feuerstein, 1980; Feuerstein et al., 2006)

These cognitive functions are developed through mediated learning experiences that occur by means of a combination of processes that actively engage both the students and the mediator (teacher). Some of these processes are:

- Exposing students to dimensions of experiences that are important for more complex thinking
- Providing students with the rationale for the elaborated instructions the mediator gives, to make them aware that they are not just carrying out a command but are actively involved in reasoning processes
- Selecting stimuli that are meaningful and establishing patterns of attention to ensure appropriate focusing behavior and, consequently, the capacity to efficiently register and correlate relevant data
- Providing models the students can imitate so that their capacity to become affected and modified through direct exposure to sources of stimulation in later life will be increased
- Repeating and varying the thinking processes so the students' interactions will become more voluntary and innovative
- Developing comparative behavior through verbal interaction (Feuerstein, 1980, pp. 20–35)

The key to IE is what Feuerstein calls "the bridging process." This refers to the mediator's deliberate connections between cognitive functions addressed in IE and disciplines to be learned.

Instrumental Enrichment is a 2-year program. It is not designed to teach but rather to provide students with the prerequisites of thinking that will enable them to derive maximum benefits from direct exposure to either formal classroom curricula or any other experience that may facilitate their learning and adaptation in life (Link, 1981). The transforming effect of using specific cognitive strategies such as IE to mediate intellectual development and learning to reverse underachievement has been confirmed by neuroscience through demonstration of the skills-based or experience-based neuroplasticity of the brain. In fact, specific cognitive tasks such as those in IE can even reverse damage in the brain (caused by both environmental factors and birth defects) and maximize the brain's neurogenesis (birth of neurons), thereby transforming the learning process itself (Holloway, 2003; Medina, 2008).

FEUERSTEIN, LIKE A TRUE DIVINER, is attuned to the interior reality of innate intelligence not readily apparent on the surface (Whyte, 2002, CD 5). His seminal theory of Structural Cognitive Modifiability provides a radical shift from a static to a dynamic process for assessing and mediating the intellectual performance of students labeled as underachieving or learning disabled. The theory makes it possible to understand the origins and the treatment of barriers to learning and thinking. His research on the effects of mediation was expanded through his effective pioneering endeavor with Down syndrome children, which proved that with mediation *all* children can succeed at intellectually demanding tasks (Jackson et al., 1998, p. 163). This understanding of modifiability and the impact of mediated learning experiences on intelligence and learning is antithetical to the belief in fixed intelligence (Dweck, 2000), disproving applicability of the bell curve to judgments about intelligence. Thus, Feuerstein has provided educators with needed support for affirming the intellectual capacity of school-dependent students.

Over the 30 years that I have been privileged to be a student of Dr. Feuerstein, I have personally witnessed the miraculous transformations that occur when students are exposed to the divining power of his work. Through my own doctoral research, I have seen the impact of IE in eliciting behaviors indicative of potential giftedness in students labeled as remedial. I have observed students at the Feuerstein Center profoundly afflicted with either Down syndrome or the loss of an entire hemisphere of their brain develop the capacity to pass standardized tests and attain professions in a variety of fields. I have witnessed the increase in achievement results of students who have had the good fortune to participate in IE through the NUA partnerships in Albany, New York, and Bridgeport, Connecticut. To date, more than 1,000 books (including, recently, Feuerstein's *Beyond Smarter*), articles, and dissertations from around the world document the transformational changes in intellectual performance and learning that continue to occur both for students identified as "special needs" (including attention deficit disorder and autism) and for mainstream underachieving students thanks to the ceaseless efforts of Reuven Feuerstein. His methods have proven that when school-dependent students are provided with prerequisite opportunities—explicit training in thinking skills, mediation of underdeveloped cognitive functions, extensive discourse in learning concepts, overt and succinct feedback, and guidance in reflection—they develop the foundations that strengthen their cognitive functioning. In this way, their intellectual capacities can be realized and optimized, and the cycle of underachievement can be replaced with accelerated achievement and self-directed learning.

We are at a tumultuous crossroad in the battle of beliefs about how to educate school-dependent students of color. If we are truly committed to ending the pernicious, unsuccessful focus on the achievement gap and replacing it with an approach that enables the innate intellectual ability of these students, we must not ignore the profound import of findings that affirm the vast intellectual capacity and resilience of the brain. Those of us in research and in the classroom must join together to demonstrate to those in power—the U.S. Congress, state legislatures, and local school boards—what research such as Reuven Feuerstein's as well as our own experience has taught us: Our students have enormous potential, but to maximize that potential we need to provide enriching mediation. Standardized testing and one-size-fits-all remediation is not the answer. We must take back the reins. We must make the effort to identify the intellectual assets of all of our students and capitalize on those strengths through mediation. In this way, our resources for innovation—our own and those of our students—can be exponentially multiplied. This is the goal, the ardent intent, to which we should apply the Pedagogy of Confidence.

5

Back to Gifted Land

Extraordinary Learning Growth Requires
Extraordinary Teaching

*Today the neurosciences bring us evidence not only of the modi-
fiability of the individual's mental functions, but also that the
changes that can be produced are in some ways (although not
yet totally defined) not merely behavioral manifestations. They
are not just changes in the structure of behavior, of the mental
processes, but are actually related to changes in both the hard-
ware and the software of the neural system. It is now no exag-
geration to state that the neural system is modified by behavior,
no less than behavior is determined by the neural system.*

—Reuven Feuerstein

---

*How are the transformational concepts synthesized from
Feuerstein's theory and methodology reflected in the
Pedagogy of Confidence?*

I am unabashedly dedicated to Reuven Feuerstein. I first met him a year
after I had finished my dissertation on applying his Instrumental Enrichment methodology to identify potential giftedness in students labeled as
"disadvantaged." It was 25 years ago, and we were in the San Francisco air-
port. We were both on our way to the same conference—he to present, me
to attend. There was no mistaking who he was. He was wearing the emblem-
atic black beret I had seen in numerous journal articles describing his
monumental divining of intellectual capacity for those who are underestimated and undervalued. When I introduced myself to him, explaining that
his methodology had been the subject of my doctoral research, he said to
me in his most professorial tone, "You must provide me with a copy while
I am here attending the conference." I called my sister and implored her to
ship a copy to me immediately, wanting to ensure that I met his charge.
Upon receiving the dissertation, I left it in the care of the hotel receptionist,
my heart pounding, anticipating the many responses a critique of his work

might elicit from him. To my utter surprise, the next morning my telephone rang and I received an anxiously anticipated—and most endearing—response from Dr. Feuerstein: "I stayed up all night reading your dissertation. Your research is much needed. We will work together." His tireless commitment to reading my dissertation that night is a metaphor for his eternal commitment to his mission. His seminal theory and methodology not only substantiated for me adopting the enrichment-type mediation fundamental to gifted education as the philosophy of my Pedagogy of Confidence, but I am privileged to be able to say that his personal mentoring, which began with that initial response to my dissertation more than 25 years ago, mediated my confidence to shepherd the design of the professional and program development activities of NUA to reflect his theory and methodology. His mentoring has also mediated my confidence to write this book.

FEUERSTEIN'S FUNDAMENTAL PRINCIPLES APPLIED THROUGH THE PEDAGOGY OF CONFIDENCE

Fifty years ago, while Feuerstein was refining his theory and methodology in Israel, Jerome Bruner in the United States was explicating what he considered the process of education, in a volume recognized as a landmark in educational theory (Bruner, 1960/1977). While efforts were being made to ramp up gifted programs, Bruner proffered advice that resonated with Feuerstein's mission and methodology:

> The new emphasis on the pursuit of excellence should not be limited to the gifted student. The quest is to devise materials that will challenge the superior student while not destroying the confidence and will to learn of the less fortunate. We have no illusions about the difficulty of such a course, yet it is the only one open to us if we are to pursue excellence and at the same time honor the diversity of talents we must educate. (Bruner, 1960/1977, p. 70)

Bruner attested that the pursuit of excellence required "long-run" and "short-run" objectives for curriculum design and instruction (Bruner, 1960/1977). This pursuit of excellence is the foundation of the Pedagogy of Confidence—the fearless expectation that all students are capable of high intellectual performance. The long-run objectives of the Pedagogy of Confidence in pursuit of excellence are self-directed learning and self-actualization. Students are motivated toward these objectives when they are supported in demonstrating high intellectual performance. Achieving this level of performance is what Bruner would identify as a short-run objective. Feuerstein affirmed the ability of all students to partake in Bruner's pursuit of excellence through his theory that the intelligence needed to demonstrate high intellectual performance is innate and can be expressed in all humans under the appropriate circumstances. For both Feuerstein and Bruner, manifesting intelligence depends not only on how the intelligence is being used but also on how it is developed (Feuerstein, 1978, 1980; Feuerstein et al., 1998, 2010; Bruner, 1960/1977). It is the development process that fuels the Pedagogy of Confidence.

Feuerstein's theory and methodology radically expanded understanding of the development of intelligence to the frontier of cognitive science. Extending this understanding to yet another frontier—that of classroom practice—requires a significant alteration of the way we assess and design pedagogy so we can amplify intelligence and maximize learning for all students, especially for those whom traditional instruction has failed. To facilitate application of Feuerstein's theory and methodology for development of transformative practice, I have distilled his salient contributions into four pedagogical considerations for reversing underachievement and eliciting the high intellectual performance that is fundamental to the Pedagogy of Confidence. These considerations have guided codification of the High Operational Practices, a key component of this pedagogy.

The first fundamental consideration for designing or selecting transformative pedagogical practices encompasses three beliefs unequivocally reflective of Feuerstein's theory of Structural Cognitive Modification:

- Intelligence is modifiable.
- All students benefit from a focus on high intellectual performance.
- Learning is influenced by the interaction of culture, language, and cognition. (National Urban Alliance, 2001)

The second consideration is acknowledgment that underachieving school-dependent students often live with debilitating circumstances caused by realities outside of school (physiological, environmental, and socioeconomic challenges, all of which affect emotional balance) as well as inside of school (marginalizing labels, assessments, and programs). These realities restrict intellectual development, causing cognitive dysfunctions that further impede learning. The third consideration is recognition that—because the brain is modifiable—enriching mediation can correct cognitive dysfunctions and strengthen the brain so that high intellectual performance can be elicited. Lastly, the fourth consideration is that mediation can be facilitated through High Operational Practices that affirm potential, provide specific training in cognitive skills that explicitly activate cognitive functions, and engage learners by bridging instruction to real-life applications that are meaningful and relevant to the students. These real-life connections cultivate a continuous direction for learning growth.

The overarching message of the four pedagogical considerations derived from Feuerstein's work is the monumental power of the process of mediation. Through mediation we can apply these considerations to transform instruction into the Pedagogy of Confidence: the artful use of the science of learning to create High Operational Practices that enable high intellectual performance. The artful aspect of the Pedagogy of Confidence is mediation. It is the interactive process the teacher employs to build confidence in students by guiding them in discussions to critically analyze tasks so that they can identify meaningful connections and applications to their personal experience. Because the teacher is guiding discovery of these personal connections, students infer that their teacher values their lived experiences, bonding the student and the teacher in the nurturing relationship that is so important for all students, but especially for students of color (Jackson, 2001).

MEDIATION AND ENGAGING LEARNING

Neuroscience research has substantiated Feuerstein's and Bruner's theories about what is needed to guarantee learning at high levels by demonstrating that learning entails strengthening connections between neurons. The brain can grow new neural connections through the skill development that occurs when enriching engagement enables students to construct meaning as they "make sense" of an experience or transform an interest into a strength. The "making sense" happens through mediation's guided, reflective discussions. The more an individual applies the skills or participates in enriching, mediated opportunities, the thicker the myelin sheath that covers the nerve axons becomes. The thicker the axon, the faster it conducts information, enabling learning to be optimized, or accelerated, and strengths to be created (Holloway, 2003, pp. 79–81). The process of learning transforms into the development of high intellectual performance through mediated experiences requiring the application of thinking or cognition at high levels, such as theorizing or hypothesizing (Bruner, 1960/1977; Feuerstein, 1978; Piaget, 1950). It is the process of making connections among experiences that counts. The brain is stimulated to make these connections through high-level tasks when it is engaged, challenged, and receives meaningful, beneficial, and compelling feedback (Jensen, 1998, pp. 32–33). This neuroscience-based description of what the brain needs for learning and high intellectual performance affirms the utility of Feuerstein's process of mediation.

The goal of Feuerstein's mediation is to rekindle in students their intrinsic personal motivation for learning by providing the strategies and opportunities that develop competence. Feuerstein stresses that refining the technique of mediation requires profound understanding of the learning process to better identify what is needed for engaging learning so that the pursuit of excellence becomes the personal goal of school-dependent students. During NUA's professional development sessions on the Pedagogy of Confidence, we conduct explicit exploration of Feuerstein's research on the learning process, substantiated by findings from other cognitive scientists and neuroscientists. To facilitate this exploration by synthesizing and translating the salient concepts inherent in mediation, we have created two symbolic representations to express the factors that affect and engage learning. These symbolic representations have proven to be extremely useful in guiding the translation of Feuerstein's theory because they clarify and simplify the optimal targets to be addressed in designing effective pedagogy and highlight the interconnectedness of culture, language, and cognition for engaging learning. The images of the representations stimulate analysis of the theory's inherent concepts, facilitating discussion from personal perspectives, interpretations, elaborations, and transfers to practice. This deep analysis and the visual images facilitate development of understanding and embedding that understanding in long-term memory (Hyerle, 2009; Marzano, 2004). In essence, these professional development sessions—in part through analysis of the symbolic representations—*use* Feuerstein's mediation techniques to *teach* Feuerstein's mediation techniques.

SYMBOLIC REPRESENTATIONS FOR PLANNING MEDIATION

The two symbolic representations employ two different modalities to illustrate two important aspects of Feuerstein's mediation technique. In the first representation, numeric and alphabetic symbols are arranged in a quasi-mathematical expression that summarizes targets to be addressed in designing effective pedagogy. The second representation is graphic, employing a Circle Map to illustrate the interconnectedness of culture, language, and cognition for engaging learning.

Targets for Engaging Learning

The expression shown below characterizes what we must do to engage learning and guarantee student success in our daily practice. It is not a mathematical formula. Instead, the symbols are shortcuts for targets gleaned from Feuerstein's objectives for mediation.

$$L: (U + M) (C1 + C2)$$
Learning: (Understanding + Motivation) (Competence + Confidence)

Understanding. Feuerstein confirmed through the Learning Propensity Assessment Device what Dewey said so many years ago: Knowledge is learned when students are engaged. Feuerstein demonstrated that students are engaged when they are actively involved and understand the concepts underlying the knowledge they are trying to acquire (Dewey, 1933; Feuerstein, 1980; Feuerstein et al., 2010). Dewey described this understanding as the ability to grasp meaning. Feuerstein explained that the brain achieves understanding as it naturally constructs meaning by perceiving relationships and by identifying and making connections to what it has experienced as being relevant and meaningful. It is these relevant and meaningful connections that engage and focus the brain to construct meaning, the major requisite for intellectual processing, understanding, and learning (Jackson, 2001). Relevance and meaningfulness are contextualized and influenced by one's culture. Our culture creates an emotionally laden frame of reference for each of us, and the way we construct meaning is affected by the interaction of our culture and our language, as these factors affect our cognition. This interaction has a profound impact on the way understanding is constructed by adolescents in general, and by school-dependent adolescents of African American descent in particular. This impact will be more extensively explicated later, in the discussion of the interconnectedness of culture, language, and cognition.

Motivation. Feuerstein pinpointed motivation as an equally important catalyst for learning. All people are intrinsically motivated to succeed (Feuerstein, 1978; Holloway, 2003; Medina, 2008; Piaget, 1950; Sylwester, 2007). When students are not motivated, the question to pursue is "What is being done to engage them and focus their attention?" Feuerstein searched to prove and address through the mediation process what Bruner opined about focusing the attention needed for motivation: "Somewhere between apathy and wild excitement, there is an optimum level of aroused attention that is ideal for classroom activity" (Bruner, 1960/1977, p. 72). The catalyst for motivation is engagement, and engagement results in focused attention. Like understanding, our engagement is affected by our brain's recognition of relevance and meaningfulness (Feuerstein, 1978, 1980; Feuerstein et al., 1998, 2010; Jensen, 1998). Developing interests and connecting to personal experiences stimulates motivation.

Mandated instruction for school-dependent students repeats what both Feuerstein and Bruner (like so many others) cited as a frequent flaw in general instruction, especially instruction for underachieving school-dependent students: little attention to understanding what stimulates motivation or applying this understanding to explicitly plan for motivating students to advance their learning and their pursuit of excellence as demonstrated through high intellectual performance (Feuerstein et al., 2010; Bruner, 1960/ 1977). Jensen (1998) has synthesized research from neuroscience that addresses this flaw, advising that motivating students is context dependent, requiring recognition of the realities that influence their lives. Jensen outlines these realities as follows: Students can be demotivated by associations from the past that provoke negative or apathetic states or past failure, unsuitable learning styles, fear of failure, irrelevant content, or lack of respect (p. 63). Practices that stimulate motivation in response to instruction include engagement, challenge, and feedback (pp. 32, 33). Conditions that foster intrinsic motivation for self-directed learning and self-actualization are positive beliefs, personal goals, and productive emotions. Goals and positive beliefs create states that release powerful pleasure chemicals in the brain, such as dopamine and natural opiates (endorphins). This pleasure reinforces the motivation for learning (p. 64). The keys to engagement for motivation for all of us are relevance, challenge, feedback, demonstrating and building positive beliefs, and guiding the development of personal goals. Positive beliefs are built through eliciting personal strengths that illustrate our ability, competence, and potential for self-actualization.

Competence and confidence. Motivation is stimulated by both a sense of competence and confidence (Dweck, 2000; Feuerstein et al., 1980; Vygotsky, 1978). Confidence is knowing what is expected and feeling you have the skills to meet those expectations. Feuerstein addresses the importance of confidence in relation to the positive impact challenge has on students when they feel a sense of competence to meet the challenge. He has demonstrated through the mediation process that confidence and competence are fortified when:

- Students are made aware of the value of their strengths and are provided the opportunity to demonstrate and apply these strengths
- Student strengths are used to develop less developed areas
- Students are made aware of the modifiability of the brain and the impact of effort and belief on modifying the brain
- Students understand the science behind the learning process
- Students feel their voices are valued and have influence in the learning process
- Students are guided to bridge their personal experiences and cultural frames of reference to concepts being taught
- Students are provided with supported challenge and feedback

• Students receive explicit training in developing their thinking and are provided opportunities to engage this thinking through inquiry and investigations that are relevant and meaningful to them (Feuerstein, 1978; Feuerstein et al., 1998, 2010; Hattie, 2009; Sylwester, 2007)

THE MEDIATION PROCESS galvanizes the attention students need for deepening their understanding, motivation, competence, and confidence. Critical components include engagement, supported challenge, and feedback. The targets garnered from mediation transform disengaging instruction into pedagogy that puts learning for high intellectual performance at the epicenter of curriculum planning.

The Interconnectedness of Culture, Language, and Cognition for Engaging Learning

I believe the most transformational influence from Feuerstein's work on pedagogical practice is his elucidation of the impact the interconnectedness of culture and language has on cognition and engaging learning. An effective symbolic representation to convey the potency of this interconnectedness is a Circle Map with a Frame of Reference (Figure 5.1). The Circle Map is one of eight Thinking Maps® created by David Hyerle. Thinking Maps are visual–verbal organizers that support the brain's natural learning processes. They assist us in identifying patterns and relationships in our thinking as well as in textual material. Thinking Maps are based on the eight fundamental cognitive processes that form the core of cognition and learning: defining a concept, describing qualities or attributes, comparing and contrasting, sequencing, classifying, part–whole relationships, cause and effect, and seeing analogies. The Circle Map is an extremely powerful tool because it enables concept development by facilitating the construction of meaning of both concrete and abstract concepts through an individual's cultural frame of reference. The simple Circle Map (without an external square) guides brainstorming of examples or thoughts related to a concept or theme. Situating the circle within a "frame" (a square) provides an added dimension—guiding the individual to put what he or she knows about a topic within his or her own frame of reference (Hyerle, 2004). The Circle Map with a Frame of Reference resembles a target because it is used to illustrate and maintain what the focus of understanding to be explored is. The concept or theme to be developed is written in the central circle, and the outer circle is used to

FIGURE 5.1   Circle Map with a Frame of Reference

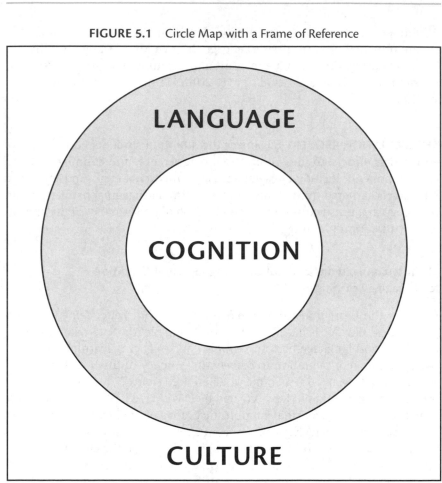

provide examples of the concept (or any information that puts the concept into context). The frame around the outside is used to generate discussion about the different experiences, perceptions, and points of view individuals have related to the concept. This discussion reveals the influence of background experience on an individual's thinking. Background experience, or cultural references, can be elicited by asking how one came to the knowledge displayed in the outer frame. But I have found that the most provocative question for developing the frame is to ask why or how the examples in the outside circle relate to or reflect the targeted concept in the central circle. This generates analytical thinking that assists in synthesizing ideas into definitions of or generalizations about the concept or theme of focus.

The responses to the questions are placed in the frame, which becomes a powerful illustration of the frame of reference of the individual.

In professional development to edify practice that nurtures high intellectual performance, cognition is targeted as the central concept in intellectual development and learning. Feuerstein has illustrated how cognition is a dominant aspect of all facets of mental processing identified by the American Psychological Association (i.e., knowledge acquisition, memory, imagery, concept formation, problem solving, decision making, critical thinking, reading, and language processing [Hyerle, 2009, p. 148]) as well as individual behavior, and it is central to adolescent learning behavior. Because cognition helps us understand and use the world around us, Feuerstein emphasizes the impact of culture on influencing cognition and perceptions of the world. Addressing this reality is a paramount focus for our investigation of the impact of culture and language on the cognition of students, especially adolescent school-dependent students of African American descent.

Adolescence is a defining point for building students' identity and confidence because it is a decisive juncture in their physiological, emotional, and cognitive development. It is a time when their engagement for learning can be maximized or demolished, contingent upon two factors: (a) the mediation they are provided to elicit cognitive agility in the formal operations they are capable of at this stage of cognitive development, and (b) the relationships teachers cultivate with them. To positively impact the cognitive development of school-dependent students of color, the cultural knowledge referenced in school must reflect who these students are—what is relevant and meaningful to them, how they see the world, and how they feel the world sees them.

Adolescent cognition and culture. Piaget theorized that the formal operational stage of cognitive development begins during adolescence (Furth & Wachs, 1974). This stage marks the emergence of the capacity to theorize about possibilities and engage in high levels of abstraction (when connected to what is familiar), hypothetical thinking, and understanding of propositions. The maturation of cognition during adolescence explains why adolescents can be reasoned with (though at times this can be quite a challenge for adults). All adolescents are capable of the maturation of formal operations, but as with all thinking and learning, environment and experience (at home, but more importantly for school-dependent students, at school) can shape the development of this type of thinking. Adolescents need explicit mediation in the application of the type of thinking inherent in formal operations for this ability to be optimally developed. With proper mediation, school-dependent adolescents can become highly adept at manifesting formal operations through a variety of high-level thinking processes, including analogous thinking, syllogistic thinking, and philosophical thinking. Without such mediation, this thinking remains underdeveloped in these individuals, impeding attainment of their full capacity for the decision making, hypothetical reasoning, dialogical thinking, and critical evaluation inherent in formal operations.

Mediating formal operations requires making cultural connections to what is to be learned. Cultural experiences create references that affect how one sees relationships and makes connections, which is why culture profoundly influences the development of formal operations. Perceiving relationships strengthens bridges between neurons. Neurons communicate through the synapses, which are junctions between nerve cells where impulses pass from one neuron to another by means of chemical signals or neurotransmitters. These bridges are activated through skill development or enriching, mediated experience that strengthens neural connections (Holloway, 2003). All cultures have their own rituals and customs that the brain recognizes as repeated experiences. These culturally generated repeated experiences create a variety of specific neural patterns (i.e., ways the synapses connect neurons or facilitate communication between them). This explains why, although all brains have the same components, they are all wired differently, and why the way we process information (our cognition) varies as well, based on our cultural experiences. The processing the wiring facilitates is manifested through intellectual behaviors, explaining why some intellectual behaviors are developed more strongly than others. The influence of culture on cognition clarifies why there are differences in what engages or enhances the learning of different individuals, a reality that must be appreciated and reflected in pedagogy in order to better engage and motivate learning. Through its impact on the development of neurological patterns, culture creates the frame of reference through which we perceive the world. This neuroscience perspective affirms why building on past experience is so important to cognitive development and the learning process.

Perceptions and emotions both emanate from personal cultural frames of reference. Emotions color the lens through which adolescents view the world, affecting every iota of the meaning they construct. This is another reality that cannot be ignored. Emotions produce chemicals that affect learning. We know that cortisol (released in response to stress) impairs cognitive functions such as creativity and comprehension, whereas dopamine and natural opiates such as endorphins (released in response to pleasure emanating from positive beliefs about self related to feelings of being valued or feelings of competence and confidence experienced from success and positive feedback) enhance motivation and learning. Adolescents are hypercharged emotionally, and the emotions of adolescents of African American descent are compounded by race-related issues (as discussed in Chapter 3), and ignoring these emotions only works against the brain's ability to learn (Jensen, 1998; Sylwester, 2007; Wolfe, 2001).

The psychological impact of emotions on adolescents generates an authentic adolescent culture, causing their ethnic cultural frame of reference to be expanded exponentially by the adolescent culture. This culture of adolescents is anchored in relationships that affect how they dress, how they think (how they infer meaning, interpret, philosophize, theorize, create syllogistic relationships, and project the future), and how they design their own unique customs.

The potency of the combination of the ethnic culture and the adolescent culture (and the emotions that steer it) elucidates why teacher–student relationships have such a profound effect on the learning and achievement of adolescents:

> Teachers who understand this recognize what they do doesn't matter nearly as much as how their students experience what they do. It's students' own experience of this behavior that is likely to have the greatest impact on their development. Results [from students] don't follow from behaviors of their teachers but from the meaning attached to the behaviors. (Kohn, 2008, p. 32)

Relationships with teachers have a formidable impact on the value adolescents put on the learning experience itself. Adolescents can discern (and are deeply affected by) teachers' behaviors that are not equitable (NICHD & NCATE, 2006). The dramatic biological changes of this period shift adolescents' self-concept and self-esteem, and they are constantly reacting to how they feel they are perceived. They increasingly compare themselves with others. Identifying their strengths, affirming their value, setting clear expectations with guiding assistance, providing feedback, and showing respect have a magnetic pull on them. Equally important, however, is their biological quest for autonomy:

> This is a time when students try to put themselves in conversations with adults who seem to have an edge over them. They slowly push the boundaries of their voices out to try to create an adult-to-adult conversation. (Whyte, 2002, CD 1)

This push is inherent in the drive for autonomy. Making punishment (from the "power over" stance) the mode of choice a teacher uses to counter the natural "push back" of adolescents' misbehavior (especially adolescent students of African American descent) succeeds only in bringing about the disintegration of motivation and productive participation in class.

During this developmental stage, confusion rather than consistency may often more accurately describe adolescent cognition and behavior, so expecting rational decisions to always be made is unrealistic. What is important to appreciate is that at this stage, even though their emotions affect their decision making, the students can be reasoned with (Sylwester, 2007, pp. 4–6). Developing a rapport so reasoning can be elicited requires creating relationships in which respect goes both ways, and thus role modeling and patience are part of the mediation process (Feuerstein, 1979a).

Connecting to adolescents' frames of reference focuses attention and facilitates the brain's use of existing neural patterns that have been strengthened by repeated use from cultural experiences. Using these neural patterns makes learning more efficient and memorable (Holloway, 2003; Jensen, 1998; Medina, 2008). When teachers are unable to make links to students' cultural references, what Kraschen (1982) described as an "affective filter" develops. When this occurs, students cannot make connections, they become unmotivated, and they are unable to identify with the teacher. Consequently, mediating the learning of new information must be situated in the immediate lives of adolescents, where relevance and meaningfulness reside for them.

The reciprocal neurocognitive interaction. Our cultural frame of reference reflects the ways that our knowledge, beliefs, and behaviors have been patterned on a neurological level. Culture is predominantly transmitted verbally, so cultural patterns are influenced by language and our language is influenced by our culture. On a cognitive level, language is a strong enculturating force that shapes our interactions and thinking. On a neurological level, language (the repeated blending of sounds, symbols, or behaviors to transmit thought or ideas) creates neural language patterns within the very structure of our brain (Feuerstein et al., 2010; Wolf, 2007). These language patterns affect how we receive and translate verbal messages, so they are also within the makeup of our cultural frame of reference—the lens through which we perceive and understand the world. How we perceive the world affects how we respond to an experience. The way we respond is considered our cognitive style. Our cognitive style is shaped by our cultural experience (Goldstein & Blackman, 1978). Adolescents have their own cognitive style, shaped by both their ethnic culture and their adolescent culture. It is the difference in cognitive styles that often causes misunderstandings, distance, or friction between students and their teachers, deeply affecting relationships, which are the very magnet for engaging adolescents, especially adolescents of color. For example, individuals of African American and Hispanic/Latino descent have been noted as having a field-dependent cognitive style. This is a style that is more socially oriented; these adolescents are engaged more by using their social frameworks for processing and structuring information. In contrast, individuals of Asian and European descent tend to exhibit a higher preference toward a field-independent cognitive style, which is a more individually oriented style (Hansen, 1997; McIntyre, 1996; Taylor & Latham-Lee, 1991). The orientation of field dependence toward more social interaction highlights why working with partners and having authentic relations with teachers is so beneficial for school-dependent students of African American descent.

Language is an inescapable element of communication in the educational setting, making a mindful approach to language a critical part of a pedagogy for engaging learning. The language of students is highly dependent on both their cultural frame of reference and their cognitive style:

> Cognitive style may also influence the communicative style or language an individual uses. Data has shown that students from African-American working-class backgrounds tend to use a style of language that may be viewed as context-dependent or characterized as language whose meaning is primarily based upon the immediate context in which it occurs. Euro-American children from a working class background tend to use context-independent language; language whose meaning is less context specific or determined independent of the context in which it occurs. (Taylor & Latham-Lee, 1991, p. 45)

Our students' culturally bound cognitive and communicative styles are their primary discourse—the way they use language, the way they think, or the way they act. The primary discourse is a way of identifying them as a member of a socially meaningful group or "social network" (Gee, 1996). Most school-dependent students of African American descent use a primary discourse that is an African-based language system, with its own phonetic, phonological, morphological, syntactic, and semantic systems (Smith & Crozier, 1998). For these students (as for most school-dependent students or English language learners), academic language is actually a secondary discourse. Secondary discourse is learned through involvement in social institutions beyond the family or social network (Gee, 1991). This means that learning academic language should be viewed in terms of second language acquisition for school-dependent students. Helping adolescents of African American descent acquire this secondary discourse requires meaningful interaction or authentic relationship-building conversation in which they perceive that they are being responded to because of the message and meaning they want to convey and not the form of their speech (Schütz, 2007). This is what engages their attention. Of course, academic language—the "sanctioned" language—must be learned too, but when students are repeatedly corrected as they are trying to engage in conversation (which is different from explicit language training), they use more, not fewer, vernacular patterns and their comprehension is stunted (Wheeler & Swords, 2006). Authentic conversation is a vehicle for language acquisition that is the more natural, effective way an individual learns language because there is genuine engagement of the student's purpose and responses. It is the search for the responses during conversation that generates the construction of meaning. Learning language through formal instruction—where the focus is more on knowledge about the language—is artificial and therefore less prone to be embedded in the memory (Gee, 1991; Schütz, 2007). School-dependent students thrive on meaningful dialogue. The key is to engage students in genuine dialogue (not lecture) relating knowledge to themselves and their world. Not only does the dialogue demonstrate the value of their responses, it also enables meaningful interaction with a wide breadth of vocabulary, promoting their language development and facility in going back and forth between their primary discourse and the sanctioned discourse modeled by the teacher. The antidote to restricted language development is authentic conversation that promotes secondary discourse to become primary discourse. Learning is contingent upon cognition and is enriched by a strong development of language.

Feuerstein has demonstrated and expounded upon another vital point in regard to the interconnection of culture, language, and cognition for school-dependent students from different cultural groups whose academic or sanctioned language development has been restricted because they have had limited opportunity for meaningful, mediated dialogue in school. Their limited development in the sanctioned language does not necessarily indicate that their cognitive abilities to comprehend using figural, symbolic, or behavioral content or their capacity for language development have been similarly restricted. Often, their cultural experiences or the cultural concepts they have learned have been conveyed through these other forms of language representation, strengthening the neural wiring produced from these forms of representation, thus making them the more efficient avenues for intellectual processing. Engaging these other forms of language representation for introducing new abstract concepts or for introducing new verbal language can be very effective for mediating learning for school-dependent students.

FEUERSTEIN HAS PROVIDED US with profound understandings about learning. These understandings are like a homing beacon that can guide the choice of High Operational Practices to mediate cognitive functioning. The High Operational Practices engage complex cognitive processes that enable high intellectual performance. Employing such High Operational Practices will ensure that we keep our promise to truly educate our school-dependent adolescent students. This education goes beyond preparing them to pass tests. This education draws out and engages their intellectual capacity, building the competence and confidence that can motivate their self-directed learning. This is the goal of gifted education that captivated me, fueled my practice, and became the heart of the Pedagogy of Confidence—extraordinary teaching to divine for extraordinary learning growth.

Applying the understandings of the structural cognitive modifiability of the brain and the interaction of culture and language on cognition to mediate learning expands and fortifies our pedagogical frame of reference. This in turn rekindles the confidence we have (which sometimes remains hidden from our consciousness) in our capacity to bestow the High Operational Practices from gifted education to our school-dependent adolescent students to inspire their competence and confidence.

6

The High Operational Practices of the Pedagogy of Confidence

*Dreaming is not only a necessary political act, but also a conno-
tation of men's and women's socio-historical form of being. There
is no change without dreams, just as there are no dreams without
hope. Belief is what generates hope; hope generates possibilities;
possibilities generate options; and options generate dreams.*

—Paulo Friere

*How are the principles of gifted education and mediation
translated into the High Operational Practices
of the Pedagogy of Confidence?*

I have learned many lessons from my time in what I call "Gifted Land." My
research and professional experiences have taught me about the pedagogical approaches and expectations that bring out the best in students labeled
as gifted. I have seen the impact of application of these techniques in students I know who attend high-performing schools in New York City (schools
such as Horace Mann and Marymount Academy), where cultivating high
intellectual performance is the modus operandi. And Feuerstein has confirmed that these *very same* pedagogical approaches and expectations are
essential components of any program for reversing underachievement and
realizing the intellectual capacity of school-dependent students.

Three compelling lessons about pedagogy for students labeled as gifted
stand out: (a) belief in and expectations for their ability drive the choices of
exposure and opportunity that are made available to them, (b) their education is designed as a constantly unfolding series of invitations to them to
explore their innate capital, the "frontier of their intelligence" (Whyte, 2002,
CD 1), and (c) the invitations they receive through their education are com-
plemented by guidance on how to apply the discoveries they make about
their intelligence so they can better determine what they want to pursue to
feel self-actualized. However, in the highly enriched environment of Gifted
Land, two pivotal realities are understated or minimized in judging the stu-

dents labeled as gifted: (a) the reciprocal relationship between the teachers' confidence and the students' success, and (b) the impact of the students' lived experiences outside and inside of school on their intellectual development, their learning, and how they are perceived. It should come as no great surprise that these same two pivotal realities are also understated or minimized in judging school-dependent students labeled as underachieving. The exposure and assistance students in Gifted Land are gifted with at home—and what school-dependent students *do not* receive at home—influence how they are judged and graded by their teachers. What clearly distinguishes the teachers in Gifted Land is that their confidence is constantly bolstered by the direction of learning growth, enrichment, and opportunities for actualization that they themselves are encouraged to make available to their students in school. These teachers enjoy elevated status thanks to their perceived success as educators, as inferred from the performance and behavior of their students—performance and behavior that have been nurtured from the experiences of mediated cultivation they receive both inside and outside of school (Feuerstein, 1979a; Feuerstein et al., 2010; Gladwell, 2008).

On several occasions during keynote presentations I have delivered, when I have identified these lessons as coming from Gifted Land, teachers from gifted programs have expressed to me that they personally take offense at what I am saying, feeling that I am denigrating gifted programs. I am always tempted to ask: To what are they really taking offense? Is it that they feel the programs are of such intrinsic value that they should not be analyzed or critiqued? Or is it that saying that school-dependent students can benefit from the methods of gifted education somehow belittles these programs? The fact that these teachers take my comments personally affirms that they view their personal success or reputation as connected to the value of the programs or to the value of the students in the programs. However, because my attention in such presentations is not focused on gifted programs themselves (that being a different discussion), but rather on gifted education as a methodology, and my intention is not to malign gifted education or the teachers in those programs (having been one myself), I do not query the reason for their distress. Instead, I make the point that having been the Director of Gifted Programs in a district as large and diverse as New York City, I find that gifted education is a pedagogical resource we can learn from to guide education for all students. The philosophy of gifted education is what all parents want for their children. And our country would benefit if we offered to *all* students what gifted education currently provides to only the few—pedagogy that elicits high intellectual performance to motivate self-directed learning and self-actualization. It is this benefit of gifted education that compelled me in my mission to substantiate its efficacy for the intellectual development and learning of school-dependent students. Evidence from the research was (and continues to be) unequivocal, which is why this philosophy forms the basis for the Pedagogy of Confidence— pedagogy for transforming educational methodology for school-dependent students so their strengths and gifts can be made apparent and cultivated.

Driven by this mission, I have codified the lessons from Gifted Land— and what is recognized as the "extraordinary" teaching inherent in gifted education—into High Operational Practices for school-dependent students that will elicit high intellectual performance from them and cultivate their self-directed learning and self-actualization. I, like so many other educators who have committed their lives to ameliorating urban education, want to stimulate the dreams these students can have for themselves and foster the belief that they can make these dreams come true.

THE HIGH OPERATIONAL PRACTICES

Four of the High Operational Practices inherent in gifted education are obvious: (a) identifying and activating student strengths, (b) eliciting high intellectual performance, (c) providing enrichment, and (d) integrating prerequisites for academic learning. Two additional High Operational Practices are less apparent, but are paramount for engaging and amplifying the learning of underachieving school-dependent students of color and are central to the mediation process. These practices are: (a) building relationships, and (b) situating learning in the lives of the students. Both of these practices show respect for the value of the students as individuals. Relationships with the students and connections to their personal lives allow them to feel that their experiences are not inferior, but rather are valuable aspects of the frames of reference from which they perceive the world. But I have learned that animating the spirit of school-dependent adolescents begs for one more critical practice that is not inherent in gifted education.

Throughout the urban districts where we at NUA have been asked to partner, one of the most gripping things we observe in the classes we visit during the initial Instructional Assessment is that intense emotions of students seem to simmer under a very insubstantial lid. We observe that these students have usually not been given opportunities to constructively share their perceptions about their schools, or the lives they live there, and they are almost never asked for input about what engages their learning. This has motivated us to include student surveys and focus groups as part of the Instructional Assessment and to include students as participants in professional development sessions. All three have provided particularly informative windows into the perceptions and emotions of these students. Through these vehicles students have clearly articulated that in classes where relationships have not been cultivated they have felt invisible or disenfranchised, never being invited to be part of the school community. These perceptions have had a deleterious effect on them as well as on those teachers who have either had their vision clouded by the stress of sanctions or distorted by student behaviors that are reactions to their personal perceptions. These teachers have not been compelled, supported, or facilitated to seek out the causes for their students' perceptions. I have also seen the incredible transformation in relationships, perceptions, participation, and performance that takes place when students are provided with opportunities for giving genuine input and receiving genuine responses to this input through dialogue and other action steps. The transformation has been so dramatic that I have included amplifying student voice for ameliorating learning and teaching as another High Operational Practice.

Thus, seven High Operational Practices are codified within the Pedagogy of Confidence:

- Identifying and activating student strengths
- Building relationships
- Eliciting high intellectual performance
- Providing enrichment
- Integrating prerequisites for academic learning
- Situating learning in the lives of students
- Amplifying student voice

These seven High Operational Practices are the axis around which the Pedagogy of Confidence revolves, gearing the objectives for each practice to facilitate students' exploration of the "frontier of their intelligence" (Whyte, 2002, CD 1) to produce the high intellectual performance that can motivate self-directed learning and self-actualization. As the teachers we work with say, "This is the new HIP HOP" (High Intellectual Performance through High Operational Practices). The high intellectual performance reflects the three beliefs gleaned from Feuerstein's theory and methodology: (a) intelligence is modifiable, (b) all students benefit from a focus on high intellectual performance, and (c) learning is influenced by the interaction of culture, language, and cognition. My listing of the High Operational Practices does not denote a prioritized order. The practices carry equal weight. However, I do purposely begin the list with "Identifying and activating student strengths" because this practice has historically received the lowest focus among practices for reversing underachievement and increasing learning of school-dependent students.

The process that galvanizes the efficacy of these High Operational Practices—shaping them to reflect the innate intellectual capacity, cognitive needs, and experiences of school-dependent students—is mediation. Mediation provides the invitation to these students for engagement and investment in their learning by addressing their frames of reference, which have been created from both their developmental realities and their ethnic cultural realities.

Mediation manifested through High Operational Practices engages the developmental cravings of adolescents by providing them with the discourse, strategies, and engagement to fulfill the innate quest to develop what Art Costa identifies as the inherent human qualities that profoundly surface during the stage of formal operations. These human qualities include metacognition, deriving meaning from experiences, reciprocal learning, problem finding, altering response patterns, constructing abstractions, inventing, storing information outside the body, and systems thinking (Costa, 2009). The mediation manifested through the High Operational Practices also values and addresses the cultural references of school-dependent adolescents. Each practice expresses six characteristics of culturally responsive teaching garnered from the abundant research of Gloria Ladson-Billings (1992, 1994) and Geneva Gay (2000). The High Operational Practices are culturally responsive in the way they are:

* *Validating:* They incorporate the cultural knowledge, prior experiences, and performance styles of students to make learning more appropriate and effective for them. They teach to and through the references and strengths of the students.
* *Comprehensive:* They develop intellectual, social, emotional, and political learning by "using cultural referents to impart knowledge, skills, and attitudes" (Ladson-Billings, 1994, p. 18). They address the whole child (cognitive, developmental, social, and emotional).
* *Multidimensional:* They address curriculum content, learning context, classroom climate, student–teacher relationships, instructional techniques, and performance assessments.
* *Empowering:* They empower students to be more successful learners. Empowerment can be described as academic competence, self-efficacy, and initiative. This empowerment is realized through attribution retraining, providing resources and personal assistance, modeling positive self-efficacy beliefs, and celebrating individual and collective accomplishments.
* *Transformative:* They develop in students the knowledge, skills, and values needed to become social critics—that is, skills involved in making reflective decisions that can be implemented in effective personal, social, political, and economic action.

- *Emancipatory:* They are vehicles for making authentic knowledge about different ethnic groups accessible to students. This knowledge expands the students' frames of reference and their recognition that knowledge is socially constructed and is something they can share in, critique, revise, and renew.

The virtue of the cultural responsiveness of High Operational Practices in engaging learning of school-dependent adolescents is obvious. These practices demonstrate the value of the strengths and cultural frames of reference of school-dependent students by making explicit how they can be capitalized on to create connections to the concepts that must be learned. I have found that teachers themselves experience benefit from employing High Operational Practices. Many have reported that they feel empowered when they observe the motivation and growth of their students and validated when they understand the breadth of the research that substantiates these practices. Appreciating the validation and affirmation the research provides, NUA's professional development sessions focus on the High Operational Practices and incorporate findings from neuroscience and cognitive science for each of the practices. (Specific examples of how teachers employ High Operational Practices are provided in Chapter 7.) The rationale for including the research in these sessions parallels an argument offered by John Medina in *Brain Rules* (2008). He maintains that one can reasonably remain "skeptical [of] any claim that brain research can without equivocation tell us how to become better teachers" (p. 4). Rather, we need to remain vigilant about continuing our own edification about the science of learning and its benefit in guiding the search for High Operational Practices that stimulate intellectual development.

THE SCIENCE OF HIGH OPERATIONAL PRACTICES

Identifying and Activating Student Strengths

Strengths are the outgrowth of interests activated by exposure and practice. Identifying and activating student strengths encourages students' belief in their potential. Years ago, B. F. Skinner and other behavioral psychologists attested that humans are more motivated by positive reinforcement that emphasizes their strengths than they are by negative reinforcement that emphasizes perceived weaknesses (Skinner, 1974). Developing an individual's strengths (or talent) provides the individual with a sense of self that is likely to motivate the individual to exhibit those strengths more frequently, leading to a reinforcing, generalizable cycle of success (Anderson, 2005).

Success generates confidence and hope, so just as Daniel Goleman (1995) has illustrated that there is an authentic biology to the effect of hope, this same biology applies to the effect of recognition of strengths. The biological effect on learning is attributed to the tightly woven interconnection among the cognitive, affective, and neurological functions of the brain.

In the neurological realm, teaching that incorporates the use of strengths optimizes the efficiency of the learning process. Like cultural patterns, strengths develop as a result of practice. Experience and practice result in fortifying connections between neurons, which makes learning using strengths more efficient (Holloway, 2003, p. 81). In the cognitive–neurobiological realm, the belief in one's potential that comes from having strengths recognized produces a sense of confidence and hope for possibilities, releasing the neurotransmitters of pleasure (endorphins and dopamine), which trigger a connection of enjoyment to learning. Thus, students are motivated to take action to participate in the learning experience, set goals for their learning, and follow through with their learning, characteristics inherent in self-directed learning and self-actualization. These pleasure chemicals also stimulate memory, another critical factor in learning (Goleman, 1995; Jensen, 1998, pp. 71–78).

The emotional impact of identifying and activating strengths in the learning process affects the reciprocal relationship between students and their teachers. Teachers appreciate the confidence their students experience from using their strengths for learning as supplementary feedback to them about their pedagogy, producing in teachers their own sense of competence and confidence, with the same neurobiological responses of pleasure and enjoyment. This reciprocal effect can transform an unproductive or even toxic classroom culture and climate to a culture of growth, with shared perspectives of possibilities from students and their teachers. Teachers realize that the identified strengths of their students validate the belief that the students do in fact have interests that have engaged them and motivated them to learn something deeply. That inference spurs belief in the capacity of the students to excel, rekindling teachers' confidence in their ability to inspire their students. The confidence stimulates them, motivating them to select experiences that are enriching and teaching practices that challenge. Believing students have potential they can nurture also diminishes the stress (and its debilitating hormones) teachers experience from the feelings of incompetence or hopelessness that are precipitated by a constant focus on weaknesses. The stress hormones are replaced by endorphins (pleasure hormones) stimulated by the observations of students' potential, making teaching more gratifying. This feeling of gratification is then manifested in behaviors (receptivity, responsiveness, energy) that make the learning experience more pleasurable for the students as well. Focusing on strengths provides a catalyst for paying attention, serves as a foundation from which to address weaknesses, and gives students a sense of commerce or self-worth.

Building Relationships

Building relationships establishes bonds that generate a positive reciprocal culture of value and possibilities. Feuerstein's research demonstrated that the most salient catalyst in modifying intelligence is the interaction or relationship between the teacher and the student. As with the identification and activation of strengths, the reason for the catalytic power of relationships on intelligence is that emotions emanating from relationships stimulate both the motivation and the memory capacity needed for learning (Feuerstein et al., 1980, 2006). Adolescence is the developmental period when relationships define a student's world, and positive and productive relationships between teachers and students can provide fertile ground for social and cognitive development (Comer, 1993; NICHD & NCATE, 2006). This is especially important for school-dependent adolescents, who search for these relationships as a magnet for drawing them to and investing them in their school. The National Longitudinal Study of Adolescent Health (a study of 90,000 middle school and high school students) found that students who feel "connected" to school (as measured by the strength and quality of their relationships with teachers and other students) are more likely to have: (a) improved attitudes toward school, learning, and teachers; (b) heightened academic aspirations, motivation, and achievement; and (c) positive social attitudes, values, and behaviors (Learning First Alliance, 2001). Possessing a deep understanding of child and adolescent development enables us to be better able to construct relationships and classroom environments that are motivational and lead to cognitive and social growth of students (NICHD & NCATE, 2006, pp. 34–35).

Eliciting High Intellectual Performance

High intellectual performance demonstrates to students their potential, which in turn motivates self-directed learning. Acts of high intellectual performance are intellectual acts that involve the application of a combination of complex thinking processes and dispositions to expand on, elaborate on, or create new knowledge, products, or ways of doing things. These processes (which include cognitive and affective skills) are driven and sustained by dispositions or Habits of Mind (Costa & Kallick, 2000). Art Costa identifies the Habits of Mind as:

- Persisting
- Managing impulsivity
- Listening with understanding and empathy
- Thinking flexibly
- Thinking about thinking
- Striving for accuracy
- Questioning and posing problems
- Applying past knowledge to new situations
- Thinking and communicating with clarity and precision
- Gathering data through all senses
- Creating, imagining, innovating
- Responding with wonderment and awe
- Taking responsible risks
- Finding humor
- Thinking interdependently
- Remaining open to continuous learning

High intellectual performance, driven by Habits of Mind, leads students to create their own intellectual and creative products or social interactions. Piaget demonstrated that high intellectual performance is generated by high-level activities that increase intellectual development (Furth & Wachs, 1974; Piaget, 1950). His theory was further proven by Feuerstein (his student), who demonstrated that intelligence is not only modifiable but can be expressed by students as high intellectual performance when they are provided with the appropriate enriching environments and methods that mediate demonstrations of learning that require high cognitive functions (Feuerstein et al., 1980, 2006). Neuroscience research has substantiated these theories through MRI and PET scans that illustrate that when the brain is engaged and encounters challenging tasks and "complex environments" supported by mediated feedback, new neural patterns are established. These neural patterns give rise to enhanced memory and intellectual behavior, and they enable high levels of performance (Feuerstein et al., 2010; Hattie, 2009; Holloway, 2003; Medina, 2008). Establishing the goal of high intellectual performance for all students transforms instruction into pedagogy that provides mediated enrichment to engage attention, motivate inquiry, cultivate creation of new ways of thinking about information, and nurture competence and confidence.

Providing Enrichment

Enrichment provides access to experiences that reinforce strengths and nurture interests that inspire personal goals for self-actualization. It is safe to say that focusing on students' weaknesses in basic skills has not been the powerful answer to reversing underachievement that we desire. Even the National Board for Professional Teaching Standards has stated that low-level content and limited teaching methods or strategies are not effective pathways for acquisition of basic skills (NBPTS, 2003). The key to generating high intellectual performance is mediated enrichment that will push students to the "frontier of their intelligence" (Whyte, 2002, CD 1). On a neurological level, enrichment literally shapes brains to be capable of doing innovative things rather than just simply repeating what other generations have done (Holloway, 2003; Renzulli & Reis, 2007). Research on the effects of enrichment on the brain has also demonstrated how it affects the cerebral cortex, where higher cognitive processing occurs, influencing both learning and behavior (Diamond, 2001).

Joseph Renzulli has spent decades championing the process of providing enrichment for generating student interests and using these interests to engage students in authentic inquiry and problem solving (Renzulli, 1975, 1982, 1983). His research on individuals classified as gifted led him to theorize that "gifted" performance starts as interests that can be cultivated through specific enrichment experiences, such as: (a) exposure through exploratory activities, (b) use of training activities to promote development of higher order thinking skills used in developing interests, and (c) providing opportunities to apply the interests in real inquiry or production. Renzulli organizes these categories of enrichment experiences into what is regarded as the hallmark of gifted education: the Enrichment Triad Model (Renzulli, 1978). (See Figure 6.1.) The Enrichment Triad has proven to be a powerful model to incorporate in pedagogy for school-dependent students because it engages and promotes creative-productive giftedness. By emphasizing the use and application of information and higher order thinking processes in an integrated, inductive, and real-problem-oriented manner, application of the model enhances understanding, motivation, competence, and confidence. It also can serve as framework for creating "identification situations" for eliciting and assessing students' strengths and "gifted behaviors" (Renzulli, n.d., pp. 1–2).

In pedagogy, mediated enrichment facilitates exposure to new experiences and information that expands the background knowledge school-dependent students need to enlarge their frames of reference and strengthen their base for inferential thinking. It enhances intelligence through the application of the critical, reflective, and creative thinking processes generated through the mediation, to promote high intellectual performance and production (Richhart, 2002). Such performance or production vitalizes intellectual dispositions such as persistence, hypothesis, elaboration, specialization, and innovation.

FIGURE 6.1   Renzulli's Enrichment Triad

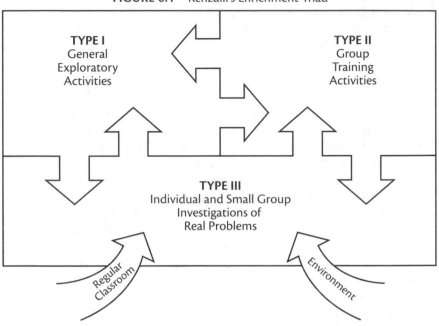

Integrating Prerequisites for Academic Learning

Integrating prerequisites into the mediation process assists in addressing cognitive dysfunctions, thus heightening understanding, competence, and confidence. Learning new concepts or complex skills depends on practice, which creates specific neural wiring that supports schema or skill formation (Holloway, 2003; Medina, 2008; SIL International, 1999). Early childhood educators understand the need to provide young students with "readiness" activities to develop the skills and conceptual understandings they need to confidently learn new skills or knowledge. Institutions of higher education understand this need as well, identifying learning needs and assigning prerequisite courses to address those learning needs. This understanding has almost been totally ignored in curriculum planning between first grade and college, leaving students ill-equipped, too often resulting in what appears to be an epidemic of learning disabilities. Poor intellectual or academic performance is directly attributed to feelings of inferiority, inefficient mental processing, and insufficient background knowledge, especially in cross-cultural situations (Comer, 1993; Dweck, 2000; Feuerstein, 1978; Feuerstein et al., 2006; Medina, 2008; Weiner, 1984). The sense of inability causes stress and anxiety, which triggers the brain to release the stress hormone cortisol, which hinders students' ability to learn (Comer, 1993; Holloway, 2003; Jensen, 1998; Medina, 2008; Sapolsky, 2003). The result is a vicious cycle of underdeveloped cognitive skills, intelligence, and ability for academic achievement. Fortunately, as Feuerstein has proven, intelligence is dynamic, and intelligence and cognitive development can be modified or transformed with appropriate interventions that can serve as prerequisites for fortifying cognitive functions and concepts necessary for learning. Neuroscience substantiates this through research illustrating the skills-based or experience-driven neuroplasticity of the brain (Holloway, 2003), demonstrating that specific types of enrichment, thinking/mental strategies, exercise-based tasks, or problem-solving activities can rewire the brain. As with the neural patterns developed through cultural rituals or the development of strengths, the resulting rewiring increases the efficiency of the mental processing or cognitive functions required for learning (Gage, 2003; Gardner, 1983/2003; Jensen, 1998; Medina, 2008). When strategies that explicitly teach cognitive skills and develop conceptual understanding are provided as prerequisite training for school-dependent underachieving students, underdeveloped cognitive functions are strengthened and high intellectual performance can be manifested.

Prerequisites arm school-dependent students with the foundation they need *before* they are assigned independent tasks, and as a result stress is reduced and new learning is optimized (SIL International, 1999). Foundational knowledge is fortified through mediated experiences that expose students to information or conceptual understandings and thinking processes in a variety of ways, enhancing their ability to discuss the information or concepts and strengthening their thinking processes for detailed elaboration in other learning situations (Feuerstein, 1978, 1979a; Feuerstein et al., 2010; Medina, 2008). Mediation of prerequisites strengthens cognitive functions for comprehension and more efficient and effective learning, thus increasing students' competence and confidence.

Situating Learning in the Lives of Students

Situating learning in the lives of students engages student participation by facilitating their discovery of relevance and meaning in academic learning. As discussed earlier, it has long been established that engaging anyone in learning requires connecting to that person's cultural context or frame of reference (Feuerstein et al., 1980, 2006; Vygotsky, 1978). Lave and Wenger (1990) extended this understanding by pointing out that learning is a function of the activity, context, and culture in which it is situated. However, most classroom learning activities that involve abstract knowledge occur out of context, hampering cognition and learning. This lack of contextualizing is an instructional reality for school-dependent students. Most often, the examples and connections they are provided come from the cultural context of the teacher or from a community to which they do not belong (Lave & Wenger, 1990). Like all students, these individuals have vast knowledge from their life experience that is organized into elaborate networks of abstract mental structures (schemata) that represent their understanding of the world. When they must assimilate new conceptions of understanding or schemata that seem to contradict their existing understandings or suppositions, they experience internal conflict, which causes them stress. This stress blocks their comprehension. Situating the new understandings in relation to their life experience enables them to recognize the connections between what is being introduced and what they already know and suppositions they have already formulated, minimizing internal conflict and maximizing comprehension (Lave & Wenger, 1990; SIL International, 1999). Working from the personal cultural context of students engages and heightens their attention because the engagements are perceived as meaningful.

Eric Jensen's work provides a neuroscience perspective on the importance of contextualizing instruction. PET scans of the brain reveal that what one recognizes as meaningful has a neurobiological correlate. Relevance and meaningfulness are a function of the brain making connections from existing neural sites to sites activated by a new experience. These connections are strengthened by emotions elicited from experience, and the emotions are triggered by the brain's chemistry (which can actually change the brain's physical structure). Context is created from prior knowledge or experiences that trigger pattern-making or relationships among neural sites. These relationships, in turn, may be related to the formation or activation of larger neural fields. The larger the neural field, the greater the possibility of connections that will create meaningfulness and relevance (Jensen, 1998, pp. 90–92).

From a cognitive standpoint, a connection from academic experiences or content to what is relevant and meaningful in students' lives captures their attention by providing the frame of reference from which to build bridges and construct meaning. The North Central Regional Educational Laboratory suggests that students are motivated to learn when curriculum considers the experiences and the issues and problems students are concerned with, as well as their patterns of processing information (NCREL, 1996). Urban school-dependent students have a powerful driving impulse for validation of their cultural frames of reference and intellectual interests. That impulse is connected to their drive for establishing individual and group presence, identity, and meaning (Comer, 1993; Mahiri, 1998). Personal culture, media, and technology have a major influence on students' frames of reference. These frames are seeded at the very epicenter of the students' cultural context and constitute the world in which they seek to creatively investigate and establish their presence, identity, and meaning. These individuals are constantly working from this epicenter to construct and communicate high intellectual performance through their contextualized "new literacies." New literacies are the social, cultural, and politically situated communication or literacy practices adolescents use outside school (Mahiri, 2004). The National Board for Professional Teaching Standards recognizes the importance of these nonschool spheres of activity and suggests that the source of high intellectual growth is not limited to traditional academic study. It can be found also in the experiences of youth outside school settings (NBPTS, 2003). Many of the literacy practices students examine and actualize outside school are "voluntary writings" or voluntary uses of literacy in the creation of original intellectual products or texts (Mahiri, 1998). Daniel Pink theorizes that this desire to demonstrate literacy through creative expression—especially telling and recalling stories from a personal cultural context—is something the brain is "hard-wired" to do. In his book *A Whole New Mind,* Pink quotes cognitive scientist Mark Turner, who suggests: "Narrative imagining . . . is the fundamental instrument of thought. Rational capacities depend on it. It is our chief means of looking into the future, of predicting, of planning, and of explaining" (Pink, 2005, p. 101). Educators who situate learning at the epicenter of their students' lives validate and connect to the driving impulse of their students. This connection heightens the students' attention and engagement, developing their competence in constructing and communicating meaning from the academic content as well as activating confidence in their creative expression.

Amplifying Student Voice

Amplifying student voice is closely linked to situating learning in the lives of students and building relationships. Making student voice part of the culture of the school encourages students to invest in their learning and in the broader school community. The practice of including student voice pro forma within the classroom and in broader school forums is designed to bring students into authentic interactions with teachers to reshape curriculum, teaching, assessment, guidance, and other matters that influence high intellectual performance and youth development. This practice prepares students to be authentic members in the Mediative Learning Community that is described in Chapter 9.

James Comer's research on child development has been at the forefront in demonstrating the link between academic success and social development.

He summarized his observations by noting that all students are born learning but need caring adults to nurture "the acquired taste" for commitment to academic success (Comer, 1993). His work illustrates how this is an especially important consideration for focusing mediation for school-dependent students who come to school with certain learning and social competencies underdeveloped yet at the same time possess rich potential for academic and social growth. For these students, the development of social behavior has not been sanctioned or even considered to be a vital component of pedagogy. The problem that is ignored is that for most school-dependent students, the cultures of their teachers and of the school are foreign to them, with mores and norms that seem alien or are outside their cultural frame of reference. This sense of alienation makes assimilating and accommodating to fit the culture of the school, while stifling their own culture, stressful (Comer, 1993; Lave & Wenger, 1990; SIL International, 1999). Students react to feelings of alienation by withdrawing or acting in ways that are regarded as "culturally unacceptable." Creating opportunities for authentically engaging students in interactions with teachers where they can voice their own perspectives and respond to the perspectives of the teachers can provide vehicles for cognitive development as well as social development. Cognitively, school-dependent adolescents (like all adolescents) are at the formal operational stage of development, and they are extremely astute and insightful. When they are provided with the proper engagement, they can move beyond surveys or focus groups (which end up being more like monologues) to become participants in genuine dialogue or discourse with teachers to analyze and intervene in real issues that have a direct impact on them. They begin to transition from an egocentric focus and to "de-center" their outlook, seeing their teachers' perspectives, enhancing their ability to think critically, synthesize, hypothesize, theorize, generalize, and determine cause-and-effect relationships regarding these issues (Feuerstein, 1978; Piaget, 1950; Sylwester, 2007). (Such participation is a major requisite of the Mediative Learning Community described in Chapter 9.) The students' voices also provide windows into their frames of reference, enabling their teachers to identify what they value and what affects how they view the world, facilitating bridges for relationships, lesson planning, and eliciting their strengths and interests.

The social development this dialogue or discourse with teachers provides has both a neurological and a cognitive base. Neuroscience has illustrated that social interactions activate "mirror neurons," which are nerve cells that produce actions that echo previously observed behaviors. Earlier it was postulated that the mirror neurons were limited to echoing motor behaviors. However, now it is believed that observation of a variety of behaviors being performed causes the observer's neurons to fire as if the observer personally was actually engaging in the behavior being observed (Medina, 2008, p. 269). Neuroscientists are finding that mirror neurons may allow us to master cultural knowledge through extensive observation (Feuerstein et al., 2010; Sylwester, 2007, pp. 3, 17–18). This means that students may be able to mirror social learning behavior and that they will have the inclination and ability to imitate such behavior when engaged in authentic discourse, augmenting and accelerating the social development of school-dependent students. This is a strong rationale for explicitly involving students in purposeful interactions with teachers. Such interactions can include attending faculty meetings or subcommittee meetings, conducting collaborative inquiry with their teachers, attending professional development and study groups, co-teaching, and co-planning student-led parent conferences. (Examples of these types of interactions are provided in Chapters 7 and 9.)

ALL STUDENTS have an innate desire for engagement, challenge, and feedback. Mediation through High Operational Practices offers the needed catalysts, encouraging the high intellectual performance school-dependent students are capable of achieving. These acts of high intellectual performance invigorate students' perceptions of themselves as competent learners while spawning positive perceptions of their teachers as facilitators of this learning. I have seen these positive perceptions create a fellowship of commitment between teachers and their students that vitalizes them both, transforming classrooms into oases of extraordinary teaching and learning.

7

The Art of Applying the
High Operational Practices

*Have you ever been so inspired that you totally forgot about all
the stumbles and walls that get in your way of achieving something great? Well that is the feeling that embodied me after my
first experience with NUA professional development. It's a sense
of empowerment and uplifting as if you have seen the "light," yet
you can't touch it quite yet. . . . I'm so moved, inspired, and motivated to learn more and deliver my learning into my teaching.
The little I was able to dabble with this last year and the little I
have done this year, is only the beginning. I KNOW, believe, and
expect great things from myself and my students. It's amazing
how some of the strategies are so simple and yet so powerful to
help students think!*

*My classroom is becoming more and more a place for fear-
lessness . . . which is my goal! My students are Champions and
with the NUA strategies delivered through High Operational
Practices, they will be able to think like one!*

—NW, Teacher, East Allen (Indiana) City Schools
(feedback from a NUA seminar)

---

*How do you integrate the High Operational Practices
into pedagogical practice?*

Integrating the High Operational Practices into a fluid pedagogy is like
composing music. Blending the various practices to create a melodic rhythm
of extraordinary teaching and learning calls for sharp attention to the goal
of the Pedagogy of Confidence—to nurture high intellectual performance.
Creating this pedagogical composition requires bringing into play knowledge of the learning process to motivate students who have experienced
years of disengagement and to help them actualize the potential they have
been made to feel they did not have. This is a complex enterprise, but as
with learning an instrument with which to play the music one composes,

faithfully exercising each practice through the artful use of strategies that express the practice builds one's competence, agility, and confidence.

Teachers and administrators in NUA's partner districts who have committed themselves to the enterprise of the Pedagogy of Confidence begin by vigilantly building on their own pedagogical repertoire. Using strategies learned in professional development sessions, they craft opportunities to orchestrate the application of High Operational Practices as the foundation of their pedagogy. Some teachers expand their repertoire slowly and methodically by cultivating one practice at a time. Others respond more exuberantly, embracing change on many fronts at once. In this chapter I present examples of how staff in the partner districts have applied the High Operational Practices. Each application described here speaks volumes about the dedication, vigilance, and innovation of these educators.

IDENTIFYING STUDENT STRENGTHS WITH THINKING MAPS

Identifying strengths has taken front stage in the business world, where recognition and appreciation of one's strengths animates individuals into productivity and allows a corporation to capitalize on harvesting the power of these identified strengths (Buckingham & Clifton, 2001). Education, especially for urban school-dependent students, is an industry that has not been as astute, either ignoring the benefits of this approach or the very reality of the strengths school-dependent students possess. Without a well-established market in education, there has been limited design of products or assessment strategies for identifying student or teacher strengths. However, a resourceful teacher does not need specialized products to identify student strengths. One only needs to invite students to reveal these strengths in a well-defined way that enables follow-up and recognition.

Two of the Thinking Maps® designed by David Hyerle are extremely effective for this purpose: the Bubble Map and the Tree Map. As was discussed in Chapter 5, the Thinking Maps are eight visual–verbal organizers that support the brain's natural learning processes. They provide a common language for teachers to use with students to assist them in identifying patterns and relationships in their thinking as well as in texts they experience (see Figure 3.1). The Bubble Map is designed for identifying and describing attributes in adjectives or adjectival phrases. It directs the user to precision in word usage for language development. The Tree Map is designed for inductive and deductive categorization and classification.

The efficacy of using these two Thinking Maps in the identification process is that not only do they trigger introspection for personally identifying strengths but they also guide students in deep reflection about how these strengths develop. In this way, students are made aware of the mechanics of the growth process entailed in building any strength and can begin to think about what might stimulate further growth. Students are also given the opportunity to discuss their strengths with their teachers, which vitalizes the relationship between them.

Teachers initiate the process of identifying personal strengths by guiding students to create their personal "portfolio of strengths," starting with a Bubble Map. Students draw their Bubble Maps, citing their strengths in adjectival form in the bubbles. The objective is for the students to identify as many strengths as possible. The next step in the process is for students to reflect on how their strengths were developed. They explicate this within a frame drawn around their Bubble Map. Students often cite who first exposed them to an activity in which a particular skill was needed, why they became interested in that skill, how they pursued developing that skill, or how that skill evolved into a strength. The purpose of the process is to bring to students' consciousness the diverse strengths they possess, the effort they applied to develop these strengths, and the abilities they have achieved as a result of the effort. The goal is to deepen their self-concept, their self-esteem, and their sense of competence while illustrating the benefits of their self-efficacy. Students are then asked to take the strengths they have referenced on the Bubble Map and classify them on a Tree Map. Through this classification they create general concepts or category headings with specific strengths under each category. (For example, they might have a category of strength labeled "Speaking" and list in that category debate, discussion, and storytelling.) Once again they are instructed to draw a frame, this time around the Tree Map. They are asked to reflect in the frame on how these categories of strengths can benefit them in school and in the outside world, how the strengths can be used productively to achieve goals they might have, and which careers might require such strengths. This reflective "strengths identification" process and making overt connections of their strengths to future career opportunities illuminates possibilities for a future of success. Seeing the strengths and potential already existing within themselves can stimulate students to increased motivation, more self-directed learning, and higher achievement—as they seek to actualize that potential.

The strengths portfolio can be expanded with the creation of another strengths Bubble Map in the middle of the year and another at the end of the year. Students share their Thinking Maps with their teachers. In this way, the maps become a tool for facilitating analysis of the students' development, changes, and growth and can provide the teacher with a deeper understanding and a more holistic view of their students. In classes where trust has been established, teachers may ask the students to share their strengths with the class so the group can collaboratively create a strengths map for the whole class. This map serves as a "Class Strengths Profile." With this map, a teacher can quickly identify commonality among strengths so strategies and activities that capitalize on those strengths can be employed on a regular basis, maximizing development of the strengths. The Class Strengths Profile also facilitates interactions for peer support (matching one student's strengths with another student's needs in collaborative projects) and grouping of students for differentiation. When faculty participate in the same process for identifying their own strengths, the school can coordinate a variety of teacher–student interactions—such as teacher–student mentorships, apprenticeships, clubs, and teacher–student collaborative inquiry projects—that can create enrichment and genuine community building inclusive of the students.

A focus on strengths animates intellectual capacity when students are able to act on their strengths by applying them and creating with them independently or interdependently (Renzulli, 1975; Renzulli & Reis, 2007). Sternberg's research substantiates what teachers experience using this process:

> By becoming aware of [student] strengths and incorporating them into instruction, educators can boost student achievement. Whether we are talking about students whose cultural background differs from the mainstream or about students whose cognitive strengths diverge from the model commonly emphasized in schools, the same principle applies: Teaching to strengths works. (Sternberg, 2006, p. 35)

ACTIVATING STRENGTHS THROUGH AFFIRMATION

Affirmation is a potent companion to identifying student strengths and interests for developing self-concept and self-esteem. It is a process of repeating one's goals or the new beliefs one wants to instill in one's subconscious mind. When students identify their strengths, these strengths can be included in affirmations that students write for themselves (autosuggestions) or that teachers write for them and students regularly repeat (heterosuggestions) (Subconscious Secrets, 2004). Positive affirmations can reprogram negative beliefs, mitigating the effect of disparaging input students receive from stereotypes, negative influences, or derogatory labeling perpetuated by a focus on weaknesses. Positive affirmations are powerful catalysts for motivating students to set goals, which is a pivotal maturation process that should be deliberately shepherded during adolescence. A study by Geoffrey Cohen of Yale University illustrated that writing affirmations for positive identity and a sense of "self integrity" near the beginning of the school year—and using them for reciting and reflecting upon during the year (especially prior

to taking a test)—raised student school performance and reduced the effects
of stereotype threat and the racially identified achievement gap by 40%
(Cohen, Garcia, Apfel, & Master, 2006; Peart, 2006).

NUA began using affirmations and "Letters of Promise" in our partnership with Newark (New Jersey) Public Schools. The Regional Director of the
Newark/NUA partnership, Ahmes Askia, knows that focusing merely on literacy skills is not a lure for engaging students. Skill training cannot touch
the heart in the way these students long to be touched—through words that
assure them that they are recognized, accepted, and supported. To demonstrate this commitment, she instituted a practice aimed at affirming the students: NUA mentors write "Letters of Promise" to the teachers and students
of the classes in which they mentor teachers. This is one such letter to students written by a NUA mentor:

> Dear Students (My *Watotos* [Swahili word for "students"]):
>
> I want you to know that your education is a civil right, and that you
> deserve the very best from those of us whom you trust to uphold this
> right. It is a civil right because as American citizens we all are entitled
> to life, liberty, and the pursuit of happiness. Life has been provided to
> us by a higher power. Liberty is an inalienable right ordained by that
> higher power. Now, with regard to the pursuit of happiness, you may
> choose this course as you like (so long as your pursuit does not infringe
> on the rights of others). Simply put, you have a right to choose to pur-
> sue the type of life that will provide you with everlasting happiness.
> I am asking you to choose to be educated! As your partner, resource,
> support, guide, mentor, coach, teacher, and advocate in this pursuit,
> I will make the following promises to you:
>
> * I promise to love you as if you were my own child;
> * I promise to expect your very best in all that you endeavor;
> * I promise to give my very best to you as your system of support;
> * I promise to care for you, listen to you, guide you, and support you;
> * I promise not to judge you for what you have done, or will do;
> * I promise to praise you when you are right, and discipline you with
>   love when you are wrong;
> * I promise to accept you for who you are, and not for who I may
>   want you to be;
> * I promise to challenge you to use your *Kuumba* (creativity) and your
>   intellectual capacity to "your" full potential;
> * I promise to provide you with the skills and fortitude to achieve at
>   high, academic levels;
> * I promise to inspire, motivate, and encourage you;
> * I promise I will keep this promise!!!

My beloved students, you are the purpose for the work of education. Your futures depend on the commitment of the entire village (parents, teachers, grandparents, siblings, friends, neighbors, and you). Please accept this letter as my pledge and promise to uphold my commitment to serve you in any and every capacity necessary to support you in your pursuit to be educated and happy.

> Peace & Blessings,
> Dr. Jay B. Marks
> (Your NUA Mentor)

Writing affirmations is now an integral strategy presented in NUA's professional development seminars on identifying and activating student strengths. The affirmation below was written for students by two teachers participating in one of our San Francisco partnership schools to bring to their awareness the belief their teachers wanted them to instill in themselves.

My Pledge of Achievement

I pledge achievement to myself
A gifted and unique intellectual
And with my community
We shall stand
Urban education
*Under H.I.P. H.O.P.
Indivisible
With equity and access for all

> —Jason Marwan Hannon & Donald Harper
> San Francisco Unified School District

*High Intellectual Performance through High Operational Practices

These two teachers have disseminated this affirmation throughout their school, and teachers and students alike now recite it on a regular basis.

Student crafting of affirmations follows identification of their strengths on Bubble Maps (as described earlier). The process, the science behind the process, and the purpose of affirmations are then discussed in class. Students often find it easier to write an affirmation for someone else first. (This lack of ease in writing personal affirmations is probably indicative of either the lack of positive mediation in explicit confidence building or the negative programming they have experienced for so long or, sadly, both.) Ultimately, the students write personal affirmations. They are guided to repeat these affirmations to themselves daily. They affix their affirmations in their notebooks or inside their lockers, or they carry them with them in their backpacks. When students and teachers write personal affirmations, their confidence is revitalized. When teachers write affirmations for their students, relationships become more profound. Additionally, teachers and students can write class affirmations, beginning each class session by reciting the affirmation in unison. Personal and class affirmations transform the class climate, increasing the sense of support and pleasure, which increases productivity.

ANIMATING STRENGTHS AND AMPLIFYING STUDENT VOICE THROUGH STUDENT-LED PARENT CONFERENCES

Students hold the key to much of what they know and are able to do. They understand their strengths and they can identify the things that challenge them. Too often however, they are the last people consulted in developing procedures or practices for the assessment of their own learning. Too often the procedures and practices we do employ to measure student learning focus on instant recall of prescribed information. Rarely do they measure what students truly understand about themselves and their learning. Rarely do students have the opportunity to reflect on their own learning and growth, and rarely are they asked to use what they know and are able to do to demonstrate that growth and understanding.

Assessment practices must create opportunities for students to connect and make sense of the pieces of their learning as well. (Smith, 1999)

Student-led parent (and guardian) conferences can provide just such opportunities, in a setting that promotes metacognition, formal operations, and mature discourse. Such conferences can serve as vehicles for facilitating mediation around meaningful, formative assessment in which students have agency in determining how they are assessed and what influence that assessment will have on the resultant path or direction constructed for them. This sense of agency—engaging in discourse around collaborative planning with a teacher, where their input is sought and valued and they receive constructive feedback—can have the power of an elixir for underachieving school-dependent adolescents, morphing disengagement and apathy into investment, reflection, and self-directed learning.

Incorporating student-led parent conferences as a conduit for amplifying student voice has been codified by a NUA lead mentor, Alexis Leitgeb, who supervised this process for several years while principal of a school in Minnesota. The key to the success of the conferences is the initial communication with parents at the beginning of the school year, explaining the conferences, how they will be conducted, the portfolio that will be devised, and the research behind the benefits of the conferences.

Throughout the semester, students compile evidence for a portfolio that demonstrates their strengths as well as areas where improvement is needed. The process is steered by a checklist of what to include, along with a rubric that provides criteria for the expected outcomes of any assignment. The students' portfolios, which will be shared with their parents, include a draft of learning goals and a script with information about their social, emotional, and physical characteristics or dispositions. When assignments are graded, students analyze and respond to their teachers about the grades they received and the work that was done; these comments also go into the portfolio.

Together, students and teachers plan the presentation of the portfolio in the parent conferences, reviewing presentation protocols through role-play and practice. The review builds competence and confidence in the process, ensuring that the students feel empowered when conducting this academic discussion with their parents.

During the first student-led conference, the teacher assists as a listener, facilitator, and troubleshooter, offering clarifications where needed for the four or five conferences happening simultaneously in the room. Students independently lead all subsequent conferences, having been trained to be listener and facilitator. The teacher remains available as a troubleshooter.

After the conference—the student's presentation and ensuing discussion with the parents—learning goals may be refined, with the plan for achieving the refined goals established in partnership among the student, the teacher, and the parents. This increases the sense of collaborative responsibility between teacher and parents in support of the student.

The final step in the process is a post-conference survey to gather parent feedback. At this point, teacher–parent conferences can also be established if a parent still has questions. However, it is important to maintain fidelity to the process to ensure that the student voice continues to carry weight.

The creation of the portfolio for the conference cultivates a "growth mindset" (Dweck, 2000), providing students with perspectives on the results of their efforts by showcasing *all* aspects of their school life. Knowing that the high intellectual performance they engage in or the intellectual products they create will be indicative of their effort, they are motivated to pay close attention to the objectives of each task and think about how best to execute achieving those objectives. Engaging in discourse about their planning for the presentation to parents—as they choose ways to forecast results, illustrate learning, and demonstrate success—stimulates development in formal operations such as hypothetico-deductive reasoning (hypothesizing and reasoning or drawing conclusions), anticipation based on projection, and innovating. Students become active, rather than passive, partners in the education process. They set goals, have voice, and improve their level of oral communication. Students with Individual Education Plans benefit from actively working with adults in setting realistic personal goals and plans for achievement. English language learners can conduct their conferences in the native language of their parents to ensure understanding.

Student-led conferences strengthen the reciprocal nature of the Pedagogy of Confidence. When students and teachers debrief together after the conferences about the success of the learning and the communication of that learning to the parents, they are both able to reflect on their strengths as well as their areas of challenge in the teaching/learning process.

BUILDING RELATIONSHIPS THROUGH MODELING

Relationships that demonstrate belief in the vast potential of school-dependent students affirm their value and stimulate their engagement. Making the practice of building relationships a keystone for an urban district requires more than affixing the goal onto a school improvement plan template. This effort, which can be herculean in districts where staffs experience a feeling of repression from the sanctions and control they have been made to endure, requires the kind of modeling from school administrators that coalesces not just the instructional staff but the entire community around this practice.

The motto of Superintendent John Ramos of the Bridgeport (Connecticut) Public Schools is "Expect Great Things." He is committed to reversing the educational inequities—spawned by poverty, immigration, and racism—that have kept many of his students stuck in a cycle of underachievement. Since 2005 he has partnered with NUA to end this debilitating cycle, and the efforts are producing results. Needed growth has begun and is accelerating. But Superintendent Ramos knows that transformation of the magnitude required demands more than professional development and instructional reform. He recognizes that this transformation demands courageously addressing the root of the word "administer": to minister service. The service required involves going beyond the boundaries of school buildings and the district office by reaching out to students and their families in their home environments, demonstrating a fearless commitment to connect with their lives in order to engage them (Jackson & McDermott, 2009, p. 36). Superintendent Ramos garners the support needed for this service to bear fruit through community advocacy.

Superintendent Ramos conducts community advocacy through what he has called the "No Excuses Campaign." The goal of the campaign has been to conduct a comprehensive assault on the high dropout rate that plagues the district by ascertaining and directly addressing the reasons students drop out. The campaign involves assembling district personnel along with community members to create teams that spend a Saturday visiting the homes of high school seniors who had dropped out to persuade them to return to school and graduate. The initial round of visits revealed a variety of realities and shed light on the lives of these students. One dominant discovery was that many parents did not actually know that their children were not attending school. Superintendent Ramos himself encountered a family living such a reality.

Arriving at the home of one of the students who had stopped attending school, Superintendent Ramos was informed by the father that his son no longer lived with him, but instead resided with the mother, leaving him unaware of his son's absenteeism. Determined to connect directly with the son, Superintendent Ramos requested the address of the mother. The father provided the address and decided to capitalize on the opportunity to make contact with his family, asking Superintendent Ramos to deliver a loaf of bread to the mother's apartment when he made his visit. Superintendent Ramos complied, likewise capitalizing on his opportunity to make a personal connection with both of the parents and their child. He informed the mother of the situation, and the son returned to school.

In other cases, although the student still lived at the address on file, the parents had no idea their child was not attending school. These parents were very grateful to have been made aware of the situation and committed to ensuring their children would return to school.

After that first Saturday, Superintendent Ramos felt that even if only one student made it back and went on to accomplish great things, the campaign would have been a success. However, what happened from the one-day event was telling. Within 2 months, 39 of the students (half of the senior dropouts) had returned to school. Parents and students alike commented on how impressed they were that the district and the community cared enough to make the unprecedented effort to come directly to their homes, demonstrating genuine concern and commitment. And from the other side, the return of so many students as a result of a one-day campaign shows the power such "ministering" can have on school-dependent students, demonstrating the desire these students and their parents have to be recognized and engaged.

ELICITING HIGH INTELLECTUAL PERFORMANCE AND PROVIDING ENRICHMENT THROUGH RENZULLI LEARNING

To reiterate the lesson of Chapter 6, strengths are the outgrowth of interests activated by exposure and practice. The more opportunity school-dependent students have for enrichment that stimulates interests, the greater will be their engagement and motivation to apply effort to develop those interests.

However, the practice of availing students of enrichment through the general instructional program appears to be most common in elementary schools. Many secondary teachers report that although they think its important to offer students enrichment experiences on a regular basis, they often feel overwhelmed. They are responsible for so many students that it is unrealistic to expect that they could have the time or access to identify resources to meet the vast range of interests of those students. Even though the Internet provides access to enrichment never before available to school-dependent students, many teachers still feel unable to shepherd the investigation of viable Internet sites. Districts now have the option of procuring the services of Renzulli Learning® to resolve this inhibiting situation. Renzulli has capitalized on the technology of the Internet to accommodate the process of identifying, supplying, and managing enrichment resources.

As described in Chapter 6, Renzulli's Enrichment Triad Model (Renzulli, 1978) provides teachers with a framework for organizing experiences that expand the interests and bolster the strengths of school-dependent students. Renzulli Learning provides an online educational profile and learning system through a search engine and profiler that match students' perceived interests, abilities, learning styles, and expression styles to thousands of enrichment activities. Students begin by completing an online profile. Their interests are then electronically matched with a plethora of resources. The basic characteristics of enrichment learning include: (a) enabling each student to select a topic that may be related to the regular curriculum or an independent topic based on his or her interest; (b) design of a product or service that is intended to have an impact on a particular audience; and (c) use of authentic methods, technological resources, and advanced-level content by the student to produce that product or service. The benefit of availing school-dependent students opportunities to develop and explore their interests extends beyond building strengths. Exploration around interests is a catalyst for inquiry and for the reading and writing that accompany that inquiry. Many students spend hours reading independently on the Internet while using Renzulli Learning. In an experimental study by Gara Field, students in a treatment group who employed Renzulli Learning were compared with students in control classes who did not have access to this resource. Students in the treatment group demonstrated statistically significantly higher growth in reading comprehension, oral reading fluency, and social studies achievement than did students in the classrooms of teachers who did not incorporate Renzulli Learning (Field, 2009).

Renzulli Learning provides a vehicle allowing students to explore possibilities for engaging their interests, building on their strengths, and expanding their frames of reference. This enrichment provides students with the opportunity to become fully participating as citizens of the 21st-century world that we as teachers and parents have promised we would make available to them.

INTEGRATING PREREQUISITES FOR ACADEMIC LEARNING THROUGH PROFESSIONAL DEVELOPMENT

In spite of the misguidance so many teachers have received as a result of the marginalizing ideology of focusing on weaknesses, millions of school-dependent students maintain a tenuous hold on hope. They desperately need educators who both believe in their potential to substantially grow intellectually and socially *and* have the tools and strategies required to bring about full expression of that belief. And there are hundreds of thousands of teachers who believe in the capacity of such students but feel ill-equipped to address their needs, especially in the case of school-dependent students of color, who are most affected by the challenges they experience inside and outside of school. To build the competence and confidence of these teachers to effectively elicit the strengths and address the needs of their school-dependent students, professional development is required that will engage them in applying the interconnectedness of culture, language, and cognition to identify or design strategies that will enhance cognitive development and motivate learning among their students.

In 2003, twelve suburban middle- and upper-middle-class school districts that encircle the city of Minneapolis joined together to create a voluntary consortium—the West Metro Education Program (WMEP)—to cooperatively address integration issues in the West Metro area. The consortium determined that just such professional development was needed if it was to bring into fruition its mission "to build the collective capacity of its members; to raise the achievement of all students; to eliminate the racial achievement gap; and to prepare all learners to thrive in a diverse world through regional leadership, integrated learning opportunities, shared resources, and mutual support" (WMEP, 1989). The leadership of the WMEP districts, through Director Mary Oberg, engaged the services of NUA to create a professional development program that would provide pedagogical strategies for culturally responsive teaching in response to the needs their urban students were manifesting in their suburban districts (Palmer & Zoffer, 2004, p. 5). They were attracted to the mission of NUA, which is to substantiate in the public schools of urban America an irrefutable belief in the capacity of all children to reach the high levels of learning and thinking demanded by our ever-changing global community. NUA's delivery model is designed to support systemic adaptability by engaging teachers and administrators in ongoing professional development (through cross-school seminars, site-based sessions, coaching, and leadership seminars) that transforms pedagogy through High Operational Practices, shifting the focus from a deficit (aka weaknesses)-based to an asset-based pedagogy: the Pedagogy of Confidence.

The additional goals articulated by WMEP and expressed through the WMEP/NUA partnership included: (a) high intellectual performance for teachers and students, (b) students becoming lifelong learners who exhibit competence and confidence, and (c) students of color being represented in activities other than those in the stereotypical areas. In the fall of 2003, the first WMEP cohort, drawn from 19 schools, committed to participating in a 2-year professional development program with NUA. In the fall of 2004, a total of 26 schools participated in the professional development program, with 17 of the original 19 schools beginning a second cohort of teachers. Throughout the sessions and site visits, teachers and administrators were exposed to a wealth of culturally relevant materials and engaged in purposeful text-based discussions regarding issues of race, ethnicity, and culture. Leadership seminars included activities to support principals in following up with their teachers between the scheduled large-group seminars and site visits.

At the end of the first year of participation, the first cohort of teachers was asked to rate the change in their abilities. The greatest areas of change were:

- Capacity to effectively address issues of culture
- Differentiated language/literacy instruction
- Monitoring students identified as "at risk"
- Skills transfer (Palmer & Zoffer, 2004)

When asked about the impact the professional development had on their planning and delivery of instruction, teachers and principals most frequently cited the following:

- More intentional use of strategies to engage more students (i.e., less "stand and deliver" instruction)
- Increased use of a common language around best practices in instruction
- Increased awareness of the impact of culture on learning and use of culturally relevant instructional materials (Palmer & Zoffer, 2004, pp. 46–48)

When asked about the impact their use of strategies delivered through High Operational Practices was having on students, participants' responses fit into two major areas of change:

- Increased motivation, engagement, and participation for students in general, and specifically among underachieving students
- Increased capacities to learn, brought about by helping students organize their thinking around common language and common strategies (Palmer & Zoffer, 2004, pp. 46–48)

In 2007, three 2-year cycles of professional development for participants were coming to an end. By this point, the number of participating schools had increased to 39. Through teacher surveys and questionnaires regarding teachers' instructional effectiveness, an outside evaluator documented significant growth in the following areas:

- Teacher capacity (to correctly replicate strategies learned)
- Pedagogy (to effectively determine the most relevant and salient application of the strategies learned)
- Regional sharing among the districts (to document effective use of strategies through student artifacts)
- Job-embedded staff development
- Curriculum development (Palmer & Zoffer, 2004)

To ensure sustainability of the impact of the partnership and to develop internal capacity for providing effective professional development, the WMEP Partner Advisory Group, with Superintendent Dan Jett, designed a 3-year Transformational Sustainability Plan (2007–2010). Implementation of this plan included creation and certification of WMEP/NUA district and school coaches. These coaches have assumed leadership in providing professional development that has maintained the integrity and outcome of the unified missions of both organizations—to provide pedagogy that reflects the irrefutable belief in the capacity of *all* students to succeed at high levels.

SITUATING LEARNING IN THE LIVES OF STUDENTS THROUGH TEACHER AND STUDENT CO-LEARNING

The pinnacle experience for students is application of their strengths and interests through collaborative production and contributions. Situating learning in the lives of students is the practice of eliciting and operationalizing their insights and strengths as bridges from themselves to understanding concepts in the various disciplines, and from those understandings to the world. The use of technology has become the epicenter of the world for many adolescents, as they develop their strength as "digital natives" for inquiry and social networking (Mahiri, 1998). In the context of the Pedagogy of Confidence, this strength can serve as a fulcrum for the practice of situating learning in the lives of adolescents. Students have been recruited as "assistant teachers" (as graduate students are in university settings) and trained to participate in the use of technology in the classroom, as well as in the planning and training of their teachers. One of the NUA senior scholars and a prolific author of books related to new literacies and urban students, Jabari Mahiri, documented just such a process of using technology to situate co-learning in the lives of students at a middle school involved in the NUA partnership in Indianapolis. He called the practice "Digital DJ-ing." The description that follows is summarized and excerpted (with permission) from Mahiri (2006):

> The Digital DJ-ing practice began as a technology project at a middle school labeled as low achieving. The low achievement record made the school eligible for the technology project, which was funded by a challenge grant and coordinated by an independent nonprofit organization for several low-performing schools in the district. The grant provided an Apple iBook laptop computer and carrying case for every student in the 6th, 7th, and 8th grades at the school. It also provided technical support for the teachers.
>
> The purpose of the grant was to apply technology as an intervention for 8th-grade students. Students were given the latitude to choose from a range of topics and formats for computer-based research and presentations on contemporary social issues. The project had to include solutions to the problems selected for research. Students could choose between PowerPoint™ and Keynote™ for their presentation formats, and their presentations had to be animated in some way. The students needed to research their topics in order to create their projects, and they were required to get feedback on their projects from peers. They would also present the projects to the whole class, and the students in the class along with the teacher would decide on the grade and on which project was the overall class winner. The class winners would compete at grade level to determine the finalist for each grade, and the finalists would eventually present their projects to the larger community of families and residents.
>
> The grant requirements included the obligation of teachers to provide documented guidance to the students in the problem-based learning experience that would be mediated by the students' use of their laptop computers. However, the teachers were not completely confident in their technical abilities to guide their students. This is why the reciprocal nature of the project was generated: Both teachers and students needed specific assistance and both had the expertise to provide that specific assistance to each other. Students mediated teachers in learning the technology and the multimodality of digital texts they chose to utilize

for their project. In turn, teachers mediated students' learning of the canons and structures of the essay format that was to be used, as well as providing guidance about the topics and sources the students could use. The grant provided the opportunity to use technology to mediate literacy and learning. Students utilized a wide variety of technological resources to sample, cut and paste, and re-mix multimedia texts for replay in new configurations, just as hip hop DJs reconfigure images, words, and sounds to play anew. The class that produced the winning project created a multitextual digital project on poverty and its connections to homelessness. The teacher reported that the brief discussions she had during mediation with these students informed her that the students' specific prior cultural knowledge about the problem of poverty influenced their selection of it as a focus.

Situating learning in the lives of these students through technology, choice, and their cultural frames of reference illuminated their perspective, their agility with multimodal texts, their creativity, and the depth and breadth of their intellectual and literacy capacities. The process facilitated development of:

- Bonding relationships between the teachers and students generated by the reciprocal mediation
- Higher order cognitive skills that resulted in the demonstration of high intellectual performance through the multimodal texts that were created
- Prerequisite training in the cognitive functions needed to strengthen and expand literacy skills

The process also shows that with proper resources teachers can be adequately supported to mediate instruction using digital resources, including support they can receive from their students.

When our perceptions and expectations expand to recognize the power of situating learning in the lives of students, we can explore the endless possibilities for creating the bridges that allow students to see connections and relationships between their world and the world we are trying to open to them (Jackson, 2001).

AMPLIFYING STUDENT VOICE

Not only do school-dependent adolescents have insights but they also have the capacity to act on these insights, as attested by the strengths and abilities teachers can elicit through high-level strategies and collaborative interactions. In fact, these students hunger after experiences that will enable them to develop the dispositions that can bring their insights into fruition. This is why amplifying student voice was codified as one of the High Operational Practices of the Pedagogy of Confidence—to give students the tools that will allow them to employ these insights as a link between academic and social development. Students are guided to share their insights and perspectives through specific protocols and various formats that bring them into conversation and action with teachers. In this way, they are acculturated to develop the discourse of school—that is, they are trained in ways of using language, of thinking, and of acting that can be used to identify themselves as members of a socially meaningful group or social network (Mahiri, 1998).

Intentional mediation to engage students in such discourse is what Annette Lareau (2003) has labeled "concerted cultivation," or the explicit and deliberate guidance of children in how to engage in interactions with adults, demonstrating and rehearsing ways to pose questions and to converse with precision and clarity. Gladwell (2008) discusses the effects of such mediation in his book *Outliers*, recounting a situation described by Lareau in which a child has been trained by his mother to develop competence and confidence in discourse with adults. In one interaction, the child "successfully shifts the balance of power away from the adults and toward himself," enabling him to be perceived as "worthy of adult attention and interest" (Lareau, quoted in Gladwell, 2008, p. 107). This is a cultural advantage not experienced by many children from poorer families, who do not receive the training at home in exercising their voice and do not have the prospect of engaging in substantive discourse with adults.

A defining component of amplifying student voice is the inclusion of students as authentic participants in professional development sessions with teachers. Participation at this level sets up discourse that engages students in the mores and discourse of learning and teaching—mores and language that would otherwise be alien to them, leaving them as cultural outsiders within their own school. Through conversations using the discourse of learning and teaching during teaming activities, teachers and students can share perspectives and gain better understanding of and appreciation for each other's cultural frames of reference. This allows them to clarify the reasons for differing points of view, which stimulates dialogical thinking and decentering of both students and teachers. The conversations also strengthen students' ability to articulate their perspectives in a language that makes them insiders, kindling a new cultural paradigm in which students and teachers are motivated to invest as co-creators and members with equal footing. Building this cultural paradigm is transformative practice that portends hope and confidence, reducing stress and fear, and activating endorphins on both sides.

Greene County Schools, Georgia

In the Greene County (Georgia) Schools, high school students participate with their teachers in professional development sessions. When the program began, the first group of students invited to take part was not composed of individuals who had been previously identified for participation. Instead, the initial cohort was made up of students who had been assigned to Saturday school detention for tardiness. One of their Saturday detention sessions happened to occur on the same day as a NUA professional development session for teachers. Being committed to the goal for inviting students to participate, Mamie Merrifield, the NUA director of the Greene County partnership, invited these students to join the teachers for the seminar. The attentiveness and fearless participation of the students—and their acceptance by the teachers—presented a significant opportunity to engage this group as the first cohort of students for the co-learning professional development that was to take place.

This kind of inclusive professional development is designed to enable teachers and students together to explore the Pedagogy of Confidence, especially culturally relevant teaching through the High Operational Practices and neuroscience research about adolescent development. The sessions are coordinated around three goals:

- *Collective mediation:* To encourage a community shared responsibility (New attendees [teachers or students] to sessions are guided by previously attending participants [teachers and students] in the learning of the content/strategies presented in the previous sessions.)
- *Culture:* To explore frames of reference and the impact they have on perceptions, teaching, and learning
- *Performance:* To collectively create modes of representing shared learning

Student feedback solicited after the first meeting was most revealing:

- "The whole process was fun. We were learning and having fun at the same time. We don't do this every day at school."
- "We are here for being tardy. I thought we would just sit there, be bored, write and be quiet until 2:00. I got on a good roll because they [the teachers] are good people showing me what I need to learn. They have a new understanding of me outside of school."
- "It was entertaining. They should be like this on a daily basis at school, not just on Saturday. I don't want to go home."

- "They are like me outside, talking and communicating with people in my environment."
- "It was fun how we got to communicate with the teachers."

During the second session, another feedback sheet was given to the students to ascertain their commitment to the process. The students were asked what they wanted as a result of participating in the co-learning with their teachers and what their perceptions of the experiences were. The following responses confirmed their commitment, recognition of their own motivation, and insight about how they felt they were being perceived:

- "To learn new things that will help with leadership and to spread what we learn to other students"
- "To learn and make learning easier and fun"
- "To be involved with other students"
- "I want to achieve and succeed in life."
- "Great things were said about us."
- "We received encouragement."

All of the students who participated in the co-learning professional development seminars ended their tardiness. They attended every session faithfully, to learn and engage with their teachers. Their teachers witnessed the transformation of these students and indeed transformed their own perceptions about the genuine care these students have about their learning and how they are perceived.

The co-learning professional development sessions have catalyzed an additional significant opportunity for the participating students for the coming school year. One of the graduation requirements for Greene County High School students is to complete a Service Learning Project. Superintendent Barbara Pulliam-Davis has authorized the creation of tutoring sessions in which students who participate in the NUA cohort can apply what they learned in the professional development sessions to tutor elementary and middle-school students. A dynamic pastor from one of the community churches mentors a group of elementary students and their parents. Under the direction of Assistant Superintendent Cynthia Brictson, NUA mentors, Greene County coaches, and high school staff, Cohort 1 students will design and deliver tutoring to this group of elementary students to fulfill the Service Learning requirement for graduation. Future ideas for the co-learning professional development include: (a) creation of NUA Student Cohort 2 by identifying students from both high school and middle school who have latent leadership strengths, and (b) bringing Cohort 1 students who have graduated or left school and may not be working or attending college back into the initiative as mentors for middle-school students.

Newark Public Schools, New Jersey

In the NUA partnership with the Newark (New Jersey) Public Schools, under the leadership of Superintendent Clif Janey, a process of training adolescents as student teachers was initiated as a component of the federally funded Striving Readers Grant for middle-school students labeled as underperforming. This program was described in an article entitled "Kids Teaching Kids" (Jackson, Johnson, & Askia, 2010) and can be summarized as follows:

> The goal of the grant is to increase literacy in the content areas. Participants include teachers of math, science, social studies, special needs, and English language learners. The professional development sessions shift the instructional focus from covering material to making sure students understand concepts, use effective learning strategies, and increase their cognitive capacities as well as their knowledge. Last year, the fourth year of a 5-year grant, students in grades 6 through 8 participated in the professional development with the specific goal of becoming student teachers collaborating with the NUA mentors to teach their classmates for the classroom demonstration component of the professional development. The students have taken the "professional development" they are receiving to great heights, displaying their strengths and commitment to learning through the collaborative lesson development they create for the classroom demonstrations. The collaborative lesson development with students team-teaching builds on the teaching and learning teachers and students have experienced during the first three years of the Striving Readers Grant. Teachers and students come to share a common language and approach to improve literacy, learning, and teaching across the curriculum. Five end-goals of the student teaching process are foci housed in the collaborative lesson planning:
>
> * High intellectual performance
> * Culturally responsive teaching
> * Student motivation
> * Classroom climate
> * Self-directed learning

The process is activated by students being selected by two or three cohort teachers through the use of "Destiny Sticks" that bear the names of all their students. After the professional development session, the selected students attend specific training with the mentor. The NUA mentor then works with the cohort teachers to determine who will be the "sending teachers" and who will be the "receiving teachers" (i.e., the teachers of classes where the students will teach). The receiving teachers give the mentor the requested skills and text for the students to teach and specify which class period would work best for the student teaching. During the training session with the students, the mentor provides them with a bank of strategies that their teachers and the mentor have taught over the past 3 years. Based on the requested skills and text from the receiving teachers, students decide which strategies they should team-teach in their lesson. The mentor teaches the students to use a Pedagogical Flow Map, an explicit instructional planning frame teachers are coached in applying during professional development sessions. (The Pedagogical Flow Map is described in detail in Chapter 10.) Students are given the opportunity to wrestle with how to design their lesson with little input from the adults. The guidance that is provided by the mentor is directed toward:

- Components of the lesson: Priming, processing, and retaining for mastery—that is, what must be done before learning (priming), what must be done during learning (processing), and what must be done at the end of the learning to push the learning into long-term memory (retaining for mastery)
- An attention signal for getting students to focus on themselves as the instructors
- Community builders to establish and maintain cooperative relationships
- Fidelity to the strategies they will teach
- The content that must be taught
- Who will be responsible for each part of the lesson
- Design of the lesson: Students are shown how to place strategies within the Pedagogical Flow Map, a 12-step sequential tool that leads the instructor to attend to each component of a lesson.
- How to use video and music in the lesson

Once the mentor or the receiving teacher introduces the student team to the class, the students teach the entire lesson. The role of the mentor and teachers is to support the students prior to the actual teaching. Observing students are introduced (by their student instructors) to strategies specifically designed to not only enhance learning but also visualize their thinking processes. Student teachers demonstrate to their peers how to create a strategy review chart from the lesson they have taught so that at a very concrete level the learning, knowledge, and understanding travel with the observing students from class to class. The strategy review chart consists sequentially of:

- Cognitive process or function of the strategy
- Name of the strategy
- Primitive (graphic if applicable, but for some strategies there is no graphic)
- Things to remember (essential points about the use of the strategy)
- Best use (priming, processing, or retaining for mastery)

This transparency, in conjunction with the NUA practice of explicit strategy instruction, helps students learn how to learn. The efficacy of this technique becomes apparent when the students begin designing their own lessons. Being aware of the purpose and process of using each strategy, they can easily design a lesson plan that most effectively meets their desired student learning outcomes.

This type of critical thinking about desired outcomes, and the ease with which the students apply it to pedagogical terminology and academic concepts is simply astounding. But the student teachers and their peers are not the only beneficiaries. Teachers realize that empowering students changes the classroom climate and situates learning in the most responsive way. Students on both sides of the demonstration lessons are engaged and motivated because the student teachers naturally design lessons that are culturally relevant for their peers. The secret to this kind of student performance is insistence on high expectations and the practice of engaging the students in the art of pedagogy by inviting them to make connections between content, curriculum design, and their own life experiences.

EACH HIGH OPERATIONAL PRACTICE steers teachers through behaviors for inspiring and nurturing high intellectual performance to motivate self-directed learning. Equally as formative to the Pedagogy of Confidence is the potency of each practice for creating a medium that reflects the competence and confidence of teachers and students individually and in harmonized reciprocity. When teachers become confident in capitalizing on each High Operational Practice, students begin to resonate to the rhythm of this confidence, eventually harmonizing with the teacher through the discovery of their own confidence and learning.

8

Namaste

The Essence of the Pedagogy of Confidence

Let's imagine creating a better world by imagining better class-rooms, where the possibilities are constantly explored of how it could be otherwise. —Maxine Greene

---

What does the Pedagogy of Confidence look like in the classroom?

Many years ago during a NUA partnership with the Indianapolis Public Schools (IPS), I had the great fortune of mentoring Audra Jordan, a second-year high school English teacher who was (and remains) the ultimate example of a teacher who exudes the Pedagogy of Confidence. What immediately bonded me with Audra was how she reminded me of myself as a teacher, passionately searching for the pedagogy that would reflect her belief in the immeasurable capacity of her students. Mentoring her allowed me to revisit my own teaching experience more objectively—and therefore more analytically. This sharpened my lens for identifying the behaviors or practices in Audra's pedagogy that engaged and expanded the learning of her school-dependent students. It was during this mentorship that I began labeling the High Operational Practices.

ORCHESTRATING THE BONDING MELODY

Audra entered teaching energized by the fire of her belief in the high intelligence and profound potential of urban students and her desire to bring forth that potential. In her second year, she was assigned to teach students scoring in the first (i.e., lowest) quartile, and she was inundated by a strangling, blinding flood of doubt and negativity about "those students" from her colleagues and others. But she did not allow the negativity to extinguish the flame of her belief. In her view, she had been gifted to have these students come into her life, for they gave her the opportunity to show them what it feels like when someone believes deeply in their capacity—to show them that her confidence in them was so strong that she would toil tirelessly to build her own competence so that she would possess the skill to elicit the full capacity they held. The confidence Audra so elegantly displayed was reciprocated by the students with the most precious gift of all—extensive learning growth—confirming that she was in fact the one for whom they had been waiting. The reciprocal relationship that was the essence of Audra's Pedagogy of Confidence reflects what is aptly described by the Buddhist concept of "Namaste." This is a reciprocal greeting that loosely translates to "The deepest part of me bows to the deepest part of you" (Chopra, 2003). The mutual honor and recognition intrinsic in such a greeting is exactly the experience urban adolescents so desperately crave and to which Audra's students so heartily responded (Feuerstein et al., 1998; Mahiri, 1998; Sylwester, 2007).

By the end of her second year of teaching, Audra's confidence had been so strengthened by her students' response to her pedagogy that she requested to remain with the same group of students for their entire high school career. She was devoted to maximizing the upward surge of their learning, and she wanted to continue her work in helping them reverse their former trend of underachievement and transform it into high intellectual performance and excellence.

WEAVING HIGH OPERATIONAL PRACTICES
INTO A PEDAGOGICAL SYMPHONY

In addition to my mentoring, Audra attended NUA professional development seminars. At each session, innovative pedagogical practices were contextualized through informative, inspirational readings such as Gloria Ladson-Billings's *The Dreamkeepers* (1994) and Lisa Delpit's *Other People's Children* (1995). Text-based discussions guided participants in analyzing their own beliefs and the practices that supported those beliefs. Audra ferociously consumed these readings, internalizing them, using them to increase the power of the lens through which she learned about her students. She knew that the depth of her identity as a successful teacher for her students would depend on the depth of her attention to their cultural frames of reference. She wanted to know what was meaningful and relevant to them, what they needed to animate their strengths and augment the skills that had been undeveloped (Whyte, 2002, CD 1). The readings enriched her appreciation of the impact of culture on cognition, and she used what she learned about her students to better situate what they were learning in their immediate lives. This practice was the key that catalyzed their creativity and talent. Audra identified the strengths her students displayed in writing when it was situated in their lives, discerning these strengths as high intellectual performance. Writing (particularly poetry, similes, and metaphors) then became the vehicle for Audra and her students to share their personal culture—those experiences that affected how they viewed the world and how they felt the world viewed them—creating the deep bonding relationships so crucial to the learning process of urban students. Audra aimed to capitalize on their writing strength to unleash other skills and dispositions, so she guided the students in making writing the way to confidently amplify their voices to express their personal philosophies and insights. She enriched their literary background by exposing them to writers beyond the curriculum, searching for works that would resonate with her students, motivating them to read further. Her pedagogy became a multimodal masterpiece. She orchestrated a mellifluous symphony that harmonized her students' voices and motivations with her belief and instructional artistry. She adroitly employed the architecture of High Operational Practices as pillars to build her pedagogy. And she choreographed prerequisites the students needed through stimulating strategies that enhanced understanding and motivated self-directed learning.

MEDIATING LEARNING

I realized through many observations of Audra that she was able to compose such pedagogical masterpieces because she was the ultimate mediator, fearlessly putting herself between what had to be learned and the students (Feuerstein, 1978; Feuerstein et al., 2010). One of the many stellar examples of this ability was the way she mediated her students' tenacity in struggling through what to them were initially arcane SAT practice exams. It was Audra's goal to instill in her students a sense of competence and confidence in their ability to go to college, in spite of all the factors that might tend to convince them otherwise. The mediation technique she innovatively employed in this case was for her to literally take the practice tests along with her students. She never looked at the answers until they were all finished. Then, together they would analyze the choices and discuss the validity of what was presented as the correct response. When there was disagreement with the answer key, the students developed cogent ways to present their arguments. Sometimes even Audra's answers did not correspond to the correct response. When this happened, the students would affectionately say, "Hey, Ms. Jordan, even you don't know the right answer?" A little banter would ensue, but the reality was undisputed: Audra's students resonated with the comfort and security she had fostered in her classroom, where everyone could always learn more and could be fearless about trying.

Audra's mediation included using the students' strengths in poetry to address undeveloped skills such as grammar and punctuation. She illustrated how each of these systems enhanced their voice, helping them get their messages across more succinctly. They investigated the power of these systems in the exemplary readings they shared, studying various grammatical and punctuation mechanics and how they affected the meaning of the texts. Investigation of ways to embellish poetry included metaphorical language such as figures of speech. Here is a poem a student wrote as a formative assessment entry following analysis and discussion of the topic "oxymoron":

Ask Me

Ask me why a sour smell surrounds the sweet smell of summer.
Ask me why our bodies are made to live forever, but some die at forty.
Ask me why I get a lump in my throat when I talk to a beautiful flower.
Ask me why the brain is far more powerful than a computer, but we are
    limited to what we use.

Assessment of the extensive writing and reading Audra motivated her students to engage in made it apparent that several students were not as adept in reading as they were in writing. Audra used the symbolic representation L: (U + M) (C1 + C2)—Learning: (Understanding + Motivation) (Competence + Confidence)—as a guide to create lessons that mediated learning prerequisite skills the students needed in order to read text independently, specifically targeting understanding and competence in language skills. Her mediation prowess was almost totally intuitive. She instinctively knew what strategies to use to develop in her students what Art Costa identified as the characteristics of a self-directed learner—self-managing, self-monitoring, and self-modifying (Costa & Garmston, 2001). She strengthened their self-managing behaviors by replacing prefabricated rubrics with exemplars of the various genres of literature they would collaboratively probe. Audra wanted her class to organically ascertain the canons of the genres to increase their understanding of what the finished product should be, hoping the deep scrutiny would etch the patterns of the genres into their memory. Metacognitive strategies were practiced, so self-monitoring became an almost immediate reaction of the students when needed. Their ability to self-modify was elevated through a daily routine of making explicit connections among the writing experiences they performed in each genre, fostering a routine of applying previously acquired learning to new tasks.

SPEAKING IN A BOLD VOICE

It soon came to my attention that the excellence Audra's students exhibited to her was rarely exhibited in their other classes. I decided to employ her practice of using poetry to amplify their voices to articulate what they felt inhibited them from demonstrating their capabilities or from having these capabilities recognized in their other classes. I asked Audra and her students to share what they felt other teachers needed to know about them and about the kind of teaching they felt was needed to engage their learning. The guiding prompt to steer the direction of their poetry was "This is what they said I couldn't . . . ; this is why I say I must . . ." Their poems were transmissions of profound insight—insight that made me smile from their brilliance while crying from the reality of the unfulfilling trajectory so many of them might be doomed to experience. This poem is a poignant example of their insight, intelligence, and competence:

> ### My Stream of Consciousness
>
> *You think that I don't know that you think*
> *I got an F because I'm lazy and indifferent.*
> *But maybe I'm just underchallenged and underappreciated.*
> *Deep down I am begging you to teach me*
> *To learn and create—not just to memorize and regurgitate.*
> *I'm asking you to help me find my own truth.*
> *I'm asking you to help me find my own beauty.*
> *I'm asking you to help me see my own unique truth.*
> *We need a miracle.*
> *One for every kid who subconsciously wants*
> *To be pushed to the edge/taken to the most extreme limits.*
> *I want you to make my brain work in a hundred different ways every day.*
> *I'm asking you to make my head ache with knowledge, spin with ideas.*
> *I want you to make my mind my most powerful asset.*
>   —S.T., 10th grade (Jackson, 2001)

This eloquent poem was written by an Eritrean American. I share that piece of information to bring attention to the fact that English was not his first language, and yet his guidance from Audra enabled him to develop an impressive command of the language.

Almost every poem was equally profound, verifying the immense talent that lay within those students who had been labeled "Quartile 1." I chose this one because it synthesized what all the students felt. When these students were in other classes, they were confronted with minimal expectations and repetitive, decontextualized, skills-building exercise books that demotivated them. Audra's practices inspired them to push their hardest, motivating the Habits of Mind that resulted in high intellectual performance. The demonstrations of their capacity fueled Audra to be a teacher of students whom she recognized as gifted, choosing strategies to challenge, support, and engage them; providing options and opportunities that would allow them to demonstrate their strengths and explore their interests; asking them to apply skills taught in writings that reflected their frames of reference and fired their creativity; and nurturing their belief and self-confidence in the possibilities that could exist for them not just as writers but as competent individuals.

Audra's confidence in her pedagogy motivated her to respond to the prompt I gave the class by expressing her own perceptions of what other teachers should know about engaging her students. She shared this poem during the "performance of the readings" of the poems in class (their class ritual), a performance that started with the students' poems and ended with Audra's. She wanted to amplify her voice to underscore what her students already knew—the depth of her commitment to their self-actualization.

Dreamkeeper

Listen to me tell you why they said I couldn't.
They said there was NO WAY
Me being Black, them being White—
Oh wait, other way around
*   See what I mean*
They said it wouldn't be possible
I'm too sensitive
Too nice
Too open
Too honest
They said I wouldn't last
Too many threats-dangers-risks
*   Oh really?*
They continued—I couldn't succeed
*   Too naïve*
*   Too Young*
TOO idealistic
There is NO WAY to save them all
*   By the Way—for future reference—Do not refer to my*
*   children as "them"*
They said I couldn't because too much damage has already
*   been done*

No motivation
Nothing to work with
    Please, I do not have time for your lies
They said I wouldn't be happy
I would become bitter, sarcastic, disillusioned
    Oh yeah? Let me know when that begins.
They said I couldn't because I'm only motivated by Anglo guilt
Races stick together
There is no way I could relate
I must be a fake, a phony
    Do you even know me?
They said I could do "better"
    But that's YOUR better—not MINE
They said I couldn't because they are the other people's children
Now listen to me tell you why I must
I must because both lives and dreams depend on it
I must because nowhere in the quote does it say that the village
    is exclusive
I must because love is round
I must because in doubting my faith, I would betray my
    innermost being
I must because it is your problem not mine
I must because neither racism, reverse racism, fear, insecurity
    nor elitism rules my world
I must because lyrical words and powerful rhythms are
    yet to be sung
I must because my passion propels me
I must because it is my daily benediction
I must because MY children, YOUR children, OUR children
They are MY laughter
MY tears
MY screams
MY TRUTH
YES MY TRUTH

I must because each of their individual faces float in and out
    of my dreams
I must because I am a natural born DREAMKEEPER
                                    —Audra Jordan (Jackson, 2001)

At the end of that year, both Audra and S.T., the student whose poem is transcribed above, recited the poems they had written those many months

earlier at the celebration that was held for all the teachers who had participated in the NUA/IPS partnership. The auditorium was filled to capacity,
but both Audra and her student confidently and boldly read their poems,
and the three of us (Audra, her student, and myself) hoped that their words
would be heeded. We hoped that their words could help change the life
trajectory not only for the students in Audra's classes but for all of the students who had so much potential and were waiting to be "pushed to the
edge" of their ability, waiting to excel. They left the stage to a standing ova-
tion, a response we hoped was a signal of possibilities for something different for these students. And for many of Audra's students something different did happen. The student who recited with her that day, S.T., went on
to Washington University in St. Louis as a journalism major and is now a
published poet.

Over a decade has passed since those mentoring years with Audra, but
the extraordinary learning growth of her students, thanks to her Pedagogy
of Confidence, is still recognized within the district. This recognition is
illustrated in a recent e-mail message from an IPS Board Commissioner
who recounted the celebration at which Audra and her student shared their
belief, their determination, and their confidence:

In a message dated 2/11/2009 12:27:42 P.M. Eastern Standard Time:

As an IPS Board Commissioner, I was there the day that we first
met Audra and her student. It was a rally/recognition for NUA and all
those teachers who were joining in the work. The exact year escapes me
as do "other" things these days; but the excitement, the connectedness
of that day were so tangible, so absolutely "ALIVE" that we were all
simply "together" with the electrifying feeling that wonderful possibilities were afoot!!!

And afoot they were. There were so many teachers present and just
brimming with eagerness, but it was Audra who walked across the stage
that day. She fairly bounced up to the podium, expressing her thanks in
being given the opportunity, encouragement, and skills she was beginning to learn from our partnership with those in the NUA.

Her passion for learning and teaching were wonderfully evident as
she introduced her student.

The young man stood before that crowd with pride and a wisdom
beyond his years as he read his poem, and we all knew that with Audra's
guidance and his talent, we had been given a look into a future unprecedented in possibility!!! And think upon the so very many students who
have been touched by the passionate engagement of Audra!!

As you can tell, that day is emblazoned upon my memory as the bal-
loons swooped everywhere, faces shined with hopeful expectation . . .

Audra routinely exercised the premise of the Pedagogy of Confidence: the fearless expectation that all of her students would learn. She knew her students harbored the potential for high intellectual performance and the desire to realize this potential. In the same way David Whyte describes "extraordinary transformation" (Whyte, 2002, CD 3), Audra had built facility with extraordinariness, optimizing her teaching through mediation that not only fostered extraordinary learning growth but also emancipated extraordinary voices and fed extraordinary strengths, which she harvested as high intellectual performance. The result was the extraordinary transformation of students who I am certain have never forgotten the culture of Namaste they were gifted to experience with a confident teacher whose identity hinged on their ability to dream and be self-actualized.

THERE ARE THOUSANDS OF TEACHERS who humbly dwell on their solitary islands of confidence, committed to not only keeping the promise to those students who long to realize their dreams—to transform their strengths into the viable means for successful futures—but to additionally opening the door of possibilities through the cultivation of strengths to inspire dreams in those for whom dreaming has been curtailed. Unfortunately, thousands of other teachers have been battered by disparaging references and repressive school climates to the point of relinquishing their roles as "dreamkeepers," succumbing to the marginalizing practices that have depleted their confidence. But scores of these teachers secretly hold on to their moral compass, searching for the methodological fuel they can surreptitiously integrate into their instruction to ignite intellectual capacity, engage learning, and just maybe rekindle their own confidence. High Operational Practices provide that fuel to empower teachers to fearlessly expect high intellectual performance and to motivate self-directed learning and self-actualization for their students and for themselves.

PART III

The Structures

9

Inspiring the Pedagogy of Confidence

Courage is not the absence of fear—it's inspiring others to move
beyond it.   —One of Nelson Mandela's "8 Lessons of Leadership"
(as reported by Richard Stengel)

What structures can be established by
school and district leadership to inspire the
Pedagogy of Confidence?

RECULTURATION AND THE ARCHITECTURE OF SUPPORT

Public school districts—such as Birmingham, Alabama; Bridgeport, Connecticut; Albany, New York; Newark, New Jersey; East Allen, Indiana; Eden Prairie, Minnesota; Greene County, Georgia; and San Francisco, California—that have chosen to embrace the Pedagogy of Confidence are distinctly different from each other. NUA has learned much from this diversity about how to customize professional development to engage teachers and develop their competence and confidence to motivate students through High Operational Practices. But the most poignant lesson learned from these partnerships is that regardless of the diverse features or issues that may differentiate the districts, they share two overarching needs. To transition their staffs and their communities from the negativity of a repressive focus on weaknesses and narrow perceptions about the potential of school-dependent students to the optimism of the strengths-focused Pedagogy of Confidence, these two critical needs must be addressed:

- The need to reculture the awareness, attitudes, and perceptions of the district staff, school board, and community within and outside of the schools (Hargreaves, 1994)
- The need to create an architecture of support structures that will coalesce all instructional staff around a uniform, integrated, and clearly articulated process for providing professional development for uncompromising high-level pedagogy

These needs are codependent: Reculturation cannot occur without an architecture of effective support structures, and an architecture of effective support structures cannot be crafted without reculturation.

The reculturation process evolves with time and fidelity, and the structures required to support the cultivation of the Pedagogy of Confidence must evolve as well. The process begins with the development of figurative structures that will inspire transformative action, and proceeds with the fashioning of literal structures that will support the mediative methodologies of the High Operational Practices. Only then can the Pedagogy of Confidence bring about the full flowering of the potential of students for high intellectual performance and academic achievement. This chapter and the next provide examples of how these two types of structures have been created in NUA's partner districts. As different as these districts are, their successes have hinged on one common factor: uncompromising, courageous commitment.

INSPIRATIONAL STRUCTURES

Guiding a Cultural Transformation from the Top: San Francisco Unified School District's Strategic Plan

Regardless of the politics, union–school district relations, or culture wherein each school operates as an independent agent, the reculturation process in all of NUA's partner districts has relied on the courageous commitment and relentless resolve of the superintendent. The fortitude these courageous superintendents exhibit emanates from their determination to be guided by their own moral compass. They have had to galvanize the support of their school boards and communities by fearlessly conveying to them that they do not perceive their schools as having an overabundance of low achievers, but instead they have underachievers with numerous strengths and vast intelligence who are dependent on their school to tap those strengths and that intellectual capacity.

This belief has been conveyed through clearly articulated goals and mechanisms that require schools to act on the goals. San Francisco Unified School District (SFUSD) has taken the bold step of enshrining this belief in a mission statement and strategic plan that enable the Pedagogy of Confidence by expressing the highest expectation that all students will have access to a "gift-ed" education that will elicit their intellectual capacities.

> The mission of the San Francisco Unified School District is to provide each student with an equal opportunity to succeed by promoting intellectual growth, creativity, self-discipline, cultural and linguistic sensitivity, democratic responsibility, economic competence, and physical and

mental health so that each student can achieve his or her maximum potential. (SFUSD, 2008)

Superintendent Carlos Garcia inspired his executive team to create a strategic plan that details the procedures and structures needed to bring this bold mission into fruition. This strategic plan, "Beyond the Talk: Taking Action to Educate Every Child Now," recognizes that specific, well-defined actions must be taken at every school to ensure that "gifted" education will be the norm for all students. Three broad goals and specific objectives established within the plan set the direction for transforming the very culture of the district:

Access and Equity: Make social justice a reality
- Diminish the historic power of demographics.
- Center professional learning on equity.
- Create an environment for students to flourish.
- Provide the infrastructure for successful learning.

Student Achievement: Engage high achieving and joyful learners
- Ensure authentic learning for every student.
- Prepare the citizens of tomorrow.
- Create learning beyond the classroom.

Accountability: Keep our promises to students and families
- Provide direction and strategic leadership.
- Create the culture of service and support. (SFUSD, 2008)

Superintendent Garcia knew that realizing these goals and objectives would depend on developing a vision that would allow people to picture the possibilities that would generate the practices. To ensure the success of his vision—and with no underestimation of the direction or the expectations he was navigating all staff to move toward—he charged his team to explicitly delineate specific student attributes the system pledged to develop through its "Vision of Student Success." This effort produced a series of commitments the district would keep to develop these student attributes, as well as a statement of the core programmatic principles of the pedagogy through which the attributes would be cultivated. NUA was invited into partnership with SFUSD to provide the professional development that would guide the pedagogy to realize the vision. This professional development coalesces around the tenets of the vision with ease because they reflect the premise of the Pedagogy of Confidence. The tenets affirm that:

- Every student who enrolls in SFUSD schools will graduate from high school prepared for the option of enrolling in a four-year college or university, pursuing a successful career, and living a healthy life.

- SFUSD students will have the confidence, competence, and information needed to make positive choices for their future and will have demonstrated strength and competence in all areas needed for full participation in the 21st-century economic, political, cultural, and intellectual life of our nation and global society. In addition to academic competency, these areas include multilingual and cross-cultural competency; technological literacy; communication skills; aesthetic sensibility; critical and creative thinking, reasoning, and solution seeking; social, environmental, and civic responsibility; and strength of character.
- SFUSD will judge itself as successful to the degree that it assists its schools, district, and community in achieving this 21st-century vision of student success for every group of students it serves. (SFUSD, 2009)

Inherent in Superintendent Garcia's vision of social justice for student achievement and accountability was ensuring that the academic playing field would be leveled for English language learners. Once again he directed development of a clearly articulated outline of commitments and programmatic principles within the strategic plan that reflected the impact of culture on cognition and that would employ reference points as directional touchstones for pedagogy. He wanted it understood that the language diversity of SFUSD students was to be respectfully acknowledged and explicitly addressed through accelerated language acquisition to optimize comprehension and learning. To meet this charge, the strategic plan includes commitments to a transformative approach that systemically uses students' languages, cultures, and experiences as the foundation for new learning and success across the curriculum, including, when possible, bilingualism, biliteracy, and multiculturalism, along with simultaneous delivery of language/literacy development through academic content instruction. These commitments have been translated into core programmatic principles that galvanize crafting methods to increase learning for all students. The methods and resources include:

- Rich and affirming learning environments
- Empowering pedagogy that uses cultural and linguistic strategies to maximize learning, access and develop student voice, and provide opportunities for student leadership
- Well-articulated, age-appropriate, challenging, and relevant curriculum that purposefully develops technological fluency, critical/creative capacities, and a full range of language, literacy, and communication

skills, including (whenever possible) bilingualism, biliteracy, and multiculturalism

- High-quality, standards-aligned instructional resources
- Valid and comprehensive assessment designed to promote reflective practice and data-driven planning in order to improve academic, linguistic, and sociocultural outcomes
- High-quality professional preparation and support to create professional learning communities of administrators, teachers, and other staff to implement a powerful vision of excellent teaching
- Powerful family/community engagement that values and draws upon community funds of knowledge to inform, support, and enhance teaching
- Advocacy-oriented administrative and leadership systems that structure, organize, coordinate, and integrate programs and services to respond systemically to student needs and strengths. (SFUSD, 2009)

This strategic plan is ambitious, but relentless ambition and unwavering direction from the top are exactly what is needed to bring about a systemic cultural shift from the traditional focus on weaknesses, which suppresses expectations for school-dependent students, to outcome-directed belief in the high intellectual capacity of *all* students. Any deviation from the direction put forth would be contrary to the transformed cultural norms the district is cultivating. The effects of the strategic plan have been strikingly apparent. Within one year after the introduction of this plan, the practices described in each school's "Balanced Scorecard" illustrated how the goals and vision of student success outlined in the strategic plan would be addressed. The course has been clearly charted and has been accepted as the best means of bringing about a resurgence of the competence and confidence needed for mining the intellectual capacities of the district's school-dependent students.

Leading as a "Soul Friend" Through Action Teams:
A Principal's Mission Realized in the Birmingham City Schools District

Although both the reculturation process and the crafting of an architecture of effective support structures must be catalyzed from the top, the process of translating High Operational Practices into high intellectual performance and academic achievement resides within the school. The critical player in vitalizing teachers to confidently adopt these practices is a confident and courageous principal. This individual must possess a courage so ferocious that it breaks down the walls of isolation constructed from the hopelessness induced by repressive policies; courage to support and inspire teachers to advocate for their students; courage to deny others justification of their deficit ideologies and practices of reducing students to statistics (Patterson, Grenny, Maxfield, McMillan, & Switzler, 2008); courage to hear and respond to the voices of the students; courage to be a "soul friend" to teachers, students, and parents alike. Being a soul friend requires getting to the heart of what matters to another. It involves creating a circle of belonging in which students, faculty, and parents feel safe to share their cultural perspectives and personal contexts, in which understanding and recognition are nourished and celebrated, and in which meaningful engagement around powerful ideas flourishes and blossoms. The account that follows (which has been drawn in part from Jackson & McDermott, 2009) describes the actions taken by a courageous and dedicated principal who well understands the importance of creating that circle of belonging.

When she became principal of Woodlawn High School Magnet in Birmingham, Alabama, in 2004, Shirley Graham knew that more than a strong administration was needed to accelerate reculturation in her school and partnership with the parents of her students. Woodlawn was a school in chaos bred from individualism, alienation, and apathy. It was in dire need of a cultural transformation that would bring together the warring factions among students and teachers vying for survival in a grab for power or status or both. Academic underperformance, disenfranchisement, and isolation characterized the student body and the staff. Prior to Principal Graham's arrival, the school had met none of its 13 goals under No Child Left Behind. She changed all of that. Armed with experience as an elementary school principal, she realized that she could not begin to seed the Pedagogy of Confidence until she had established structures that would foster relationship building and cultural responsiveness. She also realized that a "friend of the soul" does not ignore the obvious, but attacks issues head on.

On her first day on the job, Principal Graham was greeted by a bevy of angry parents, the media, and halls full of students who did not have schedules. One of the first actions she took after this encounter was to acknowledge the parents' frustrations, asking them if they would be willing to work with her in a Parent Action Team. Principal Graham brought support to the Action Team concept through the school's partnership with the Church of the Highlands, whose philosophy supports building communities with teachers, students, and parents. The church assists parents by providing classroom tutoring and donating useful resources such as classroom supplies for every teacher; it also offers instruction in parenting skills for young mothers and provides mentoring for male students (Jackson, Long, & Merrifield, 2010).

Principal Graham next formed a team of previously disenfranchised department and school leaders, empowering them to do the jobs they had been hired to do and more. She has worked tirelessly with her staff and students to encourage them to see the merits of culturally responsive interactions. Her ability to optimize teachers' practices, especially when it comes to staff ownership of professional development and the sustainability of professional development efforts overall, remains a key to improved student achievement. Principal Graham has incorporated leadership seminars and large group seminars through a NUA partnership to demonstrate strategies and provide opportunities to practice building community and being culturally responsive. Each summer, she hosts summer faculty retreats. These retreats prepare teachers for the upcoming school year and present new material that facilitators have learned at the NUA Summer Academy. In addition to highlighting the teacher leadership, mentoring, and sustainability efforts under way at Woodlawn High School, Principal Graham can point to upward trends in the school's assessment data. These improvements can be at least partially attributed to the professional development focus of the school and the ways in which the school culture has begun to transform (Jackson et al., 2010).

Principal Graham took similarly insightful actions with students, guiding their participation in a variety of activities that developed a sense of community and provided student recognition. By the 2005–2006 school year, the school had met 10 of its 13 goals, including the one for mathematics. The following year it met all of its goals and achieved adequate yearly progress in reading and math. Since then it has continued to maintain these gains and more. Woodlawn students are now competing and excelling in academic bowls and math derbies. High achievement among the students has also been displayed districtwide: In the 2009–2010 Birmingham City Schools District Science Fair, Woodlawn students won Second Place in Environmental Science and Second and Third Places in Physical Science. Woodlawn students have also excelled in the humanities and social sciences, winning Third Place in the Birmingham City Schools Black History Oratorical Contest and Second Place in the Urban League Essay Contest.

Principal Graham assumed the role of friend of the soul and all around her have reaped the rewards. For her staff, her students, and their parents, she has modeled understanding, couching expectations in the lived context of the receiver, and getting to know faculty and students deeply and nonjudgmentally. Her Action Teams have became vehicles for dialogue, leadership, and shared decision making. At Woodlawn, Principal Graham has built a community in which the African concept of *"ubuntu"* dominates— that sense that I am who I am because of whom we all are.

Sustaining the Momentum:
Coaches' Seminars in the City School District of Albany

Establishing the Pedagogy of Confidence in a school or in a district does not happen overnight. From the first tentative steps, the process is an odyssey of dedicated effort to bring about the essential reculturation and create an architecture of support structures. Administrators and teachers must coalesce to support each other in learning and applying new practices. Momentum builds as their confidence grows and they begin to see their efforts bear fruit in the form of high intellectual performance by their students. To sustain the momentum and expand the reach of the new pedagogy, these first implementers must assume leadership to inspire their colleagues to join them in their odyssey.

NUA's professional development programs feature a sustainability plan that enables schools and districts to continue the work on their own. In the City School District of Albany, New York, district coaches who have participated in NUA's Summer Academy have zealously pledged to mediate the Pedagogy of Confidence into the norms for their schools. Together they plan opportunities to elaborate on and extend professional development around the Pedagogy of Confidence. They create vehicles for sharing ideas and practices throughout their schools, and they promote methodologies for identifying and developing student strengths and acknowledging high intellectual performance. Under the leadership of the district's Director of Coaching, Connie McNally, the coaching team resolved to center their sustainability plan on the design and delivery of monthly districtwide professional development seminars, which they called "PDExpress." To garner support from their district leadership and generate teachers' interest in participating in the seminars, the team produced an innovative video commercial to be aired on the district's internal cable station. They created a lively script for the video around the titles of the professional development sessions they would be presenting in the district. Each session was represented by a short skit portraying the concept of the session. These included:

- *Building Community:* Embedding meaningful and relevant community builders into pedagogy
- *Bloomiaget:* Combining Bloom's Taxonomy and Piagetian principles
- *Making Magic with Maps:* Using Thinking Maps® together to guide students in creating strong writing products
- *You've Been Framed:* Connecting to students' frames of reference to ensure relevance and high levels of thinking
- *Turn No into Thank You:* Employing various high-level strategies to encourage conflict resolution

- *Accelerate, Not Remediate:* Learning how to apply High Operational Practices to enrich and accelerate learning
- *Why Ask Why?* Using high-level questioning to promote higher intellectual performance
- *Which Way Do We Go?* Aligning high-level strategies to instructional needs
- *Celebrate:* Sharing artifacts and successes from the past year to expand the community of learning

The commercial was aired throughout the Albany school district, garnering the support the team needed from district officials and their colleagues. One of the team members enthusiastically e-mailed me after the first session:

> Hi Yvette!
>
> The school year has been busy, but is off to a great start! . . . I am excited to report that we did our first district-wide professional develop-ment on Community Builders and it was a success! Our next one is in 2 weeks. Teachers have been going to PDExpress to sign up for the other seminars that we are offering! We work well as a team!   KA

The team has been affirmed and inspired, and its members are now even more deeply pledged to continue their leadership in the odyssey to instill the Pedagogy of Confidence throughout their district.

IMMENSE DESIRE exists within districts and schools to transform practices in a way that will bring out the full potential of students and increase the career satisfaction of teachers. The Pedagogy of Confidence can set these educators on just such a transformational path. Inspirational superintendents and principals can create the atmosphere and ignite the spark that will spur them to action. Dedication and the energizing effect of success will propel them along the course their moral compass has dictated.

10

Mediative Structures

We shape ourselves to fit this world, and by the world we are shaped again. Each of us wishes to become visible, wishes to be heard, wishes to be seen.

—David Whyte

What structures facilitate the Pedagogy of Confidence to seed and flourish?

I have seen the energy that is catalyzed by inspirational structures become contagious, transforming teachers and principals into confident agents of change. These educators come to realize that this change runs deep—they are no longer the same. They can no longer acquiesce in perpetuating practices that have failed their students. They become committed to an educational philosophy and practices that will bring out the very best in every one of their students. They confidently follow their moral compass (Whyte, 2002, CD 1).

Personal transformations such as this are unequivocally articulated again and again in NUA professional development sessions. As teachers share artifacts from their own classrooms that illustrate their application of High Operational Practices or high-level strategies, they describe the transformation in their practice and in their thinking. They contrast their new approaches with their old: "My old self used to do _____ this way [explaining the former practice], but my new self does it this way [explaining the new]."

The continuous reflection teachers experience when they embrace the Pedagogy of Confidence motivates them to search for structures that will transform how they do business in even more extensive ways. Establishing mediative structures in two areas is especially important:

- Development of instructional techniques that will optimize the literacy prowess of students, as the key to enabling their academic learning
- Creation of an environment within the school community that makes students feel they are invested members, working in concert with their teachers to maximize development of their own strengths

These mediative structures are discussed in the pages that follow.

MEDIATING DISCIPLINE LITERACY AND LEARNING
FROM WRITTEN TEXT: THE PEDAGOGICAL FLOW MAP

Confident teachers of school-dependent students aim to empower them. There is no denying that literacy is the key to students' success in school, a fact that is illustrated dramatically in scores on standardized assessments. Tragically, for too many school-dependent students, these very scores trigger the repressive remedial instruction that catapults them into an ever more precipitous downward spiral. One of the most staggering pieces of data I have encountered in my work with secondary teachers is that 65% of their students fail one or more subjects each term. What is disturbing is the way this statistic is often regarded as a simple fact of life. Even more disturbing is the failure to recognize the fundamental and paramount reason for this devastating statistic: In traditional secondary instruction, reading and learning achievement are codependent processes. Poor performance and lack of engagement in any subject area can be traced back, in large part, to poor comprehension of discipline-related text. Schools labeled as low performing have grappled with this problem through remediation-type programs, and when the programs fail—as they almost invariably do—blame is heaped on the students for their "lack of motivation." The reality is that secondary students must be able to read to learn, and when they cannot read, they do not have the tools to construct meaning from text—so they cannot learn subject matter. This is the platform upon which their disengagement resides.

Dedicated teachers are well aware of the codependency of reading and learning, yet underachieving students are still most often relegated to narrowly focused remediation instead of the type of tutoring or broad enrichment support advantaged students receive outside of school. Out of frustration and fear for their jobs, teachers succumb to the sanctioned mode of instruction—teaching from textbooks. They admit that 90% of what they use to teach their students is written text, even though the textbooks often repel the students, rarely containing references to their personal experiences or to world affairs unfolding daily. And standard textbooks only infrequently—if at all—take advantage of the digital modes of communication students use every day to stay informed and to make contact with their peers. Sadly, many of the teachers who are so wedded to textbooks also uncomfortably admit that 50–60% of their students cannot read the textbooks they are using. Thus, they are unable to complete independent assignments, and many do not even try. And they fail—fail at learning, fail on assessments, and fail in climbing out of the intellectual hole in which they find themselves. Surveys of students conducted in association with NUA's Instructional Assessments reveal, however, that most of them do care very much about succeeding, as S.T. declared so eloquently in his poem in Chapter 8. They simply have not received mediated training in the skills they need to succeed. Teacher surveys reveal that the teachers recognize this, but they do not know how to make learning from reading happen for these students (Jackson, 2002, p. 1). The result is that, like the students, too many teachers approach the teaching and learning experience with a lack of competence and confidence. The difference is that the teachers' shortcomings are easier to mask and discount, and so their lack of competence has gone unrecognized or has been ignored—and thus has persisted.

If 90% of what is used to teach is written text, then—even though they are not reading teachers—teachers in the other disciplines must become teachers of text comprehension if students are to learn. Text comprehension in the various disciplines requires not only basic reading skills but also "literacy" in the discipline in order for students to effectively read and assimilate the associated text. Attaining this literacy entails developing a frame of reference related to the discipline that enables students to shift their adolescent perspective to the perspective of the textbook author. This can be an extremely difficult process because it involves understanding the technical language or lexicon of the discipline, being comfortable with the organizational structure that is used for presentation of the material (e.g., science, history, and literary texts each have their own characteristic structural patterns), and finding personal experiences to relate to the experiences being referenced in the text. All of these factors affect the comprehensibility of the text and, therefore, the learning of the content within that text that is possible. To become competent learners in several disciplines, students must develop a reading dexterity that adapts to the use of skills and text structures esoteric to each discipline, as well as a breadth of background knowledge that creates the different foundations from which they infer meaning.

The significance of proficiency in the literacy of the various disciplines is made obvious through achievement standards for those disciplines. The standards highlight the specific understandings and skills required within specific areas of learning. As discussed in Chapter 5, when standards are analyzed across disciplines, it becomes clear that the skills required are not restricted to epistemic or esoteric skills. In fact, they are predominantly cognitive skills. Standardized assessments in the various disciplines are designed to alert us to the progress students are making in grasping the understandings from the disciplines and in applying knowledge and indicated skills. Analysis of both the standards and the assessments from the various states reveals that the standards can be narrowed, or compacted, down to three learning expectations and targets for instruction. These are:

- Fluency in the lexicon or language of the specific disciplines of learning
- Ability to construct meaning from text from the disciplines or areas of learning
- Ability to communicate the meaning constructed from the text

Engaging the learning of school-dependent students to stimulate them to develop proficiency in the literacy of the various disciplines is an imperative of the Pedagogy of Confidence. The symbolic representation L: (U + M) (C1 + C2)—Learning: (Understanding + Motivation) (Competence + Confidence)—described in Chapter 5 is the guide for accomplishing this. In the context of engaging learning in the literacy of the disciplines, the components of the representation may be translated as follows:

- *Understanding (U)*: Grasping understandings of the concepts inherent in the disciplines
- *Motivation (M)*: Develops when bridges are built between the disciplines and what is meaningful and relevant to the students (their frames of reference)
- *Competence (C1)*: Dexterity with the skills identified in the standards related to constructing and communicating meaning in the disciplines, especially fluency in the lexicon and comprehension skills needed for content acquisition through text and language
- *Confidence (C2)*: Develops when students understand, are motivated, and become competent in the skills required

This symbolic guide serves as the basis for the mediative planning structure formalized in the Pedagogical Flow Map.

The Purpose of the Pedagogical Flow Map

Dexterity in all types of reading, but especially academic reading, can be bolstered through mediation that is guided by the symbolic representation described above. However, effectively and efficiently designing this mediation can be a daunting task for teachers. Even with professional development in these experiences, secondary teachers express the need for an explicit structure that can assist them in mediating learning needs while guiding students to learn from texts. This need can be met with the mediative planning structure called the Pedagogical Flow Map (PFM; see Figure 10.1). The PFM addresses the "what" (the standards of the disciplines and content acquisition) and the "how" (engagement and enhancement of reading expertise) of academic achievement through literacy in the disciplines. The

FIGURE 10.1 Pedagogical Flow Map

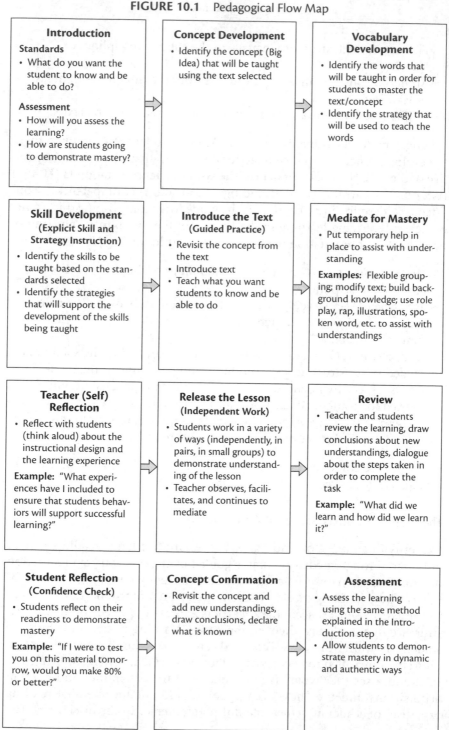

Introduction

Standards
- What do you want the student to know and be able to do?

Assessment
- How will you assess the learning?
- How are students going to demonstrate mastery?

Concept Development
- Identify the concept (Big Idea) that will be taught using the text selected

Vocabulary Development
- Identify the words that will be taught in order for students to master the text/concept
- Identify the strategy that will be used to teach the words

Skill Development
(Explicit Skill and Strategy Instruction)
- Identify the skills to be taught based on the standards selected
- Identify the strategies that will support the development of the skills being taught

Introduce the Text
(Guided Practice)
- Revisit the concept from the text
- Introduce text
- Teach what you want students to know and be able to do

Mediate for Mastery
- Put temporary help in place to assist with understanding

Examples: Flexible grouping; modify text; build background knowledge; use role play, rap, illustrations, spoken word, etc. to assist with understandings

Teacher (Self) Reflection
- Reflect with students (think aloud) about the instructional design and the learning experience

Example: "What experiences have I included to ensure that students behaviors will support successful learning?"

Release the Lesson
(Independent Work)
- Students work in a variety of ways (independently, in pairs, in small groups) to demonstrate understanding of the lesson
- Teacher observes, facilitates, and continues to mediate

Review
- Teacher and students review the learning, draw conclusions about new understandings, dialogue about the steps taken in order to complete the task

Example: "What did we learn and how did we learn it?"

Student Reflection
(Confidence Check)
- Students reflect on their readiness to demonstrate mastery

Example: "If I were to test you on this material tomorrow, would you make 80% or better?"

Concept Confirmation
- Revisit the concept and add new understandings, draw conclusions, declare what is known

Assessment
- Assess the learning using the same method explained in the Introduction step
- Allow students to demonstrate mastery in dynamic and authentic ways

PFM ensures alignment with the High Operational Practices of the Pedagogy of Confidence. In short, this means that instruction will be designed around the development of cognition that leads to high intellectual performance.

The PFM is a Flow Map template for planning an instructional unit. The unit represented in the PFM may involve one or more lessons and may take one day, several days, or longer to complete. A Flow Map is one of the eight Thinking Maps® created by David Hyerle (see Figure 3.1), and it expresses a series of steps in a process. Each step in a PFM represents a critical element of effective instructional planning in mediating the literacy of a discipline; combination of the steps can produce high-powered teaching. Three objectives of the PFM lead to the mediation it provides: (a) to enable students to reach an independent level of reading text, (b) to enable students to learn from text, and (c) to motivate ideas for self-directed learning and independent investigations for creating intellectual products in which learning is applied and demonstrated.

Six critical elements of the PFM guide the mediation process:

- *Clear instructional goals:* Steer purposeful, adept ordering of the PFM steps to accomplish the intended instructional purposes
- *Focus on learning:* Directs preparation, mediation, pauses for review and reflection, provision for practice, and assessment
- *Concept or theme:* Anchors the unit, bridging what is relevant and meaningful to students and vocabulary development
- *Process as well as content:* Focuses attention on the thinking and learning processes in which students might be engaged, as well as the content they will learn
- *Text-oriented learning:* Facilitates responding to text (includes written, oral, figural, symbolic, performing arts)
- *Ongoing reflection and discussion:* Ensures adjusting activities as needed for maximum effect

The Steps Involved for Mediation

There are 12 steps in the PFM. In some units, each can be clearly identified as a separate step; in others, various steps may be combined. Although some steps usually come before others, the order is not fixed. Steps may be ordered and adjusted in a number of ways, depending on the teacher's instructional goals and purposes. The objective of each step is implied in the essential question presented.

Each of the steps of the PFM plays a vital role in an effective instructional unit, but the critical feature that makes the PFM a vehicle for mediation is that it is explicitly shared with the students at the beginning of the unit. Every step can then become a focus for discourse. The purpose of the discourse is to build confidence, letting students know: (a) what the expected outcomes are, and (b) how the teacher has thought about arriving at those outcomes. The PFM is displayed during the entire instructional period for the unit. In this way, not only do students constantly know where they are in the process but, most importantly (and this is the zenith of mediation through a PFM), they learn to use the PFM to identify when misunderstanding or confusion sets in. Students and the teacher employ a protocol that involves the students alerting the teacher when they are no longer "getting it," and the teacher responding by asking at which point on the PFM they last understood the lesson. The students indicate this point, and the teacher determines a different way of mediating understanding. The process provokes sharp attention and metacognitive analysis on the part of the students and a change in perspective from the lens of the teacher to lens of the learner. This shift in viewpoint spurs the teacher into discussion specifically aimed at identifying what might be causing confusion or blocking understanding, and subsequent consideration of what other approach the teacher might take for mediation. The discussion also serves as the catalyst for dialogical thinking on the part of the students, helping them gain a better understanding of the teacher's perspective. One powerful end product of this collaborative approach is the mutual appreciation developed between teacher and students about learning and teaching, strengthening the understanding, motivation, competence, and confidence of all parties, which serves to deepen their reciprocal bond.

Introduction. The introduction serves an orienting function. The teacher identifies the goals of the lesson, the nature of the knowledge to be studied, and the demonstrations of understanding that students should be able to complete at the end of the unit (Richhart, 2002). In preparing the introduction, the teacher anticipates and plans for guiding students in developing the dispositions or Habits of Mind (Costa & Kallick, 2000) that will be needed for motivating their high intellectual performance, self-directed learning, and independent investigations or intellectual products related to the unit.

Concept Development. Almost all instruction is most effective when it is connected to a broad concept to which students can readily relate. Identifying a core concept for the unit helps the teacher focus on promoting learning rather than simply covering content. The teacher helps students construct meaning from a place of strength by artfully making connections to their cultural references or prior experience and knowledge from within their frames of reference. These connections provide entry points for engaging or creating student interests through exposure to enriching experiences and extensive dialogue. Enriching, engaging experiences could include exposure to audio and video resources, websites, virtual experiences, discussions with professionals from the field, visits to sites exemplary of the discipline, and so forth. These exposures give students the chance to expand their background knowledge, and thus facilitate inferential thinking (Renzulli, 1994). The extensive dialogue generated during this step can break down the "cognitive wall" many students hit around the 5th grade. (Pogrow explains the cognitive wall as the inability to connect concepts to other experiences. He postulates that it results from a lack of enriching conversation needed to build strategic understanding. Without such conversation, students cannot develop the cognitive structures to which ideas or concepts can be linked or from which they can be expanded. When students hit this wall their motivation is deflated, their learning is restricted, or they react through what are considered resistant behaviors [Pogrow, 2000].)

Vocabulary Development. Knowledge of the lexicon of a discipline is critical for constructing meaning and achieving deep understanding of the content of that discipline. Students' vocabulary is strengthened and expanded when they are guided to make associations from the key concepts for a lesson or within the discipline to terminology found in the text or associated with the concept (e.g., synonyms, antonyms, figurative language, etc.). Explicit introduction of associated vocabulary within a discipline, including word morphology and etymology, accelerates development of fluency and comprehension.

Skill Development. Virtually all instructional units provide opportunities to help students develop language skills, number skills, or cognitive skills, and it is important to identify what skill or skills might be developed in any given instructional unit. In some units, the skills are best taught at the beginning, before students proceed with the unit. In others, skills are best taught at the end, after students have a context for skill development. In still other units, skills may be the main focus of a lesson that forms part of a larger instructional unit.

Note: The concept, vocabulary, and skill development steps each offer a portion of the anticipatory set or prerequisite background underachieving students may need to enable them to read the text independently (Hunter, 1994).

Introduce the Text. At this point, the teacher revisits the concept of the text and navigates the connection between the concept and the content to be learned. Identifying the content to be learned and the strategies that will help students learn keeps the instruction focused and purposeful, drawing students' attention to what will be the relevant details.

Mediate for Mastery. Even when instruction has been effectively designed and adeptly implemented, some students may not gain the expected understandings right away. More often than not, the teacher will need to provide additional reference texts (audio, video, websites, virtual tours, etc.), demonstrations, activities, and so on to ensure that all students master the content.

Teacher (Self) Reflection. This is the point in the lesson when the teacher confirms that students are ready to independently read the text and engage in independent or group activities. The teacher makes this judgment by reflecting with the students about the learning experience thus far and the features that have been built into the unit to support the students' learning success. The shared model of self-reflection offers the opportunity for dialogical thinking (hearing the teacher's perspectives) and provides additional entry points for further clarification or for development of new perspectives and insights.

Release the Lesson. In this step, differentiated activities can be provided. Students engage in opportunities to independently practice and apply what they have learned in a variety of ways that allow for demonstrations of understanding leading to high intellectual performance and creation of intellectual products. The teacher observes, facilitates, and continues to mediate as necessary.

Review. At some point after the initial teaching, students are guided to review what they have learned. Students can review in several ways, including sharing what they pursued independently during the "Release the Lesson" segment of the unit. Through the review, teachers prod students for conclusions about their new understanding.

Student Reflection. Student reflection may involve a self- or peer-check on understanding or a judgment about being ready for an assessment. In addition, students may be invited to think about personal references they could make and what they have learned about themselves as learners after concluding the unit study. This PFM step can readily be combined with others. For example, students can be invited to reflect on what they have learned when they are confirming their understanding of the central concept or theme of the lesson.

Concept Confirmation. Students are mediated through different opportunities to think again about the core concept that was the focus of the instructional unit. The purpose of this rethinking is to have students confirm their understanding of the concept, cite concept-oriented details from the text and the instructional activities, share personal references, and express any further insights or conclusions.

Assessment. At the end of the instructional unit, assessment is used to determine whether students have met the instructional goals. Assessment allows students to demonstrate their understanding of concepts and information and to display any skills they may have acquired. The assessment may be formative (leading directly to additional instruction) or summative (as a culmination for the unit). Application of learning to high intellectual performance or independent investigations leading to intellectual products provides a powerful means for demonstrating real understanding of the content. A simple recitation of facts on a final exam is a far less effective method of assessing real learning.

Teachers' responses such as the two that follow confirm the confidence they develop in mediating their students' comprehension and illustrate how they engage their students through use of the PFM. Even the earliest attempts can be rewarding:

March 2010

> The Pedagogical Flow Map has revolutionized the way I teach! As a result of the implementation of my first PFM (attached), my students went so much deeper into the text than usual and were highly engaged throughout the novel. The most beautiful moment, however, occurred after we read the novel and the students were preparing their final projects. I was assisting a student with his work when I looked up and realized that EVERY student was focused, engaged, and working. This has never happened. I have had numerous struggles this year keeping my students involved. It almost brought a tear to my eye!
>
> I am aware that my Pedagogical Flow Map may need some work; I am sure there are corrections and clarifications that need to be made. However, I do know this . . . I am on a roll!!!!
>
> Thanks for listening!

C.R.

East Allen City Schools, Indiana

As teachers' confidence grows, so too does their willingness to share their PFMs during professional development sessions. The ensuing discussions demonstrate how the PFMs can be mediative structures in any discipline. Two examples of PFMs are shown in Figures 10.2 and 10.3. These clearly illustrate the competence teachers have developed in artfully selecting strategies for engaging and maximizing the learning of their students.

FIGURE 10.2 Pedagogical Flow Map for a Lesson on Measurement

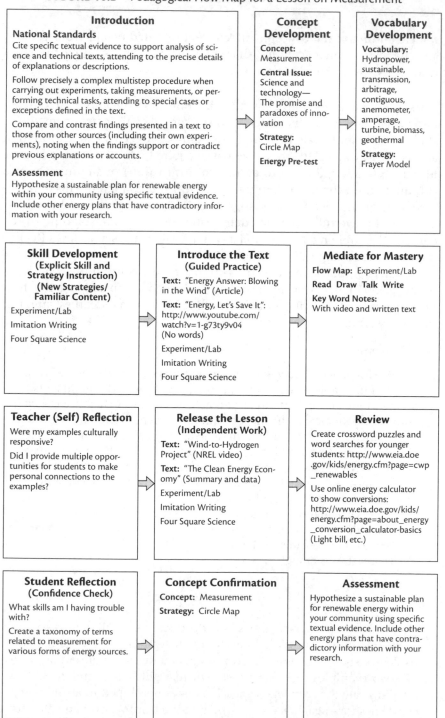

Introduction

National Standards

Cite specific textual evidence to support analysis of science and technical texts, attending to the precise details of explanations or descriptions.

Follow precisely a complex multistep procedure when carrying out experiments, taking measurements, or performing technical tasks, attending to special cases or exceptions defined in the text.

Compare and contrast findings presented in a text to those from other sources (including their own experiments), noting when the findings support or contradict previous explanations or accounts.

Assessment

Hypothesize a sustainable plan for renewable energy within your community using specific textual evidence. Include other energy plans that have contradictory information with your research.

Concept Development

Concept: Measurement

Central Issue: Science and technology— The promise and paradoxes of innovation

Strategy: Circle Map

Energy Pre-test

Vocabulary Development

Vocabulary: Hydropower, sustainable, transmission, arbitrage, contiguous, anemometer, amperage, turbine, biomass, geothermal

Strategy: Frayer Model

Skill Development (Explicit Skill and Strategy Instruction) (New Strategies/ Familiar Content)

Experiment/Lab

Imitation Writing

Four Square Science

Introduce the Text (Guided Practice)

Text: "Energy Answer: Blowing in the Wind" (Article)

Text: "Energy, Let's Save It": http://www.youtube.com/ watch?v=1-g73ty9v04 (No words)

Experiment/Lab

Imitation Writing

Four Square Science

Mediate for Mastery

Flow Map: Experiment/Lab

Read Draw Talk Write

Key Word Notes: With video and written text

Teacher (Self) Reflection

Were my examples culturally responsive?

Did I provide multiple opportunities for students to make personal connections to the examples?

Release the Lesson (Independent Work)

Text: "Wind-to-Hydrogen Project" (NREL video)

Text: "The Clean Energy Economy" (Summary and data)

Experiment/Lab

Imitation Writing

Four Square Science

Review

Create crossword puzzles and word searches for younger students: http://www.eia.doe .gov/kids/energy.cfm?page=cwp _renewables

Use online energy calculator to show conversions: http://www.eia.doe.gov/kids/ energy.cfm?page=about_energy _conversion_calculator-basics (Light bill, etc.)

Student Reflection (Confidence Check)

What skills am I having trouble with?

Create a taxonomy of terms related to measurement for various forms of energy sources.

Concept Confirmation

Concept: Measurement

Strategy: Circle Map

Assessment

Hypothesize a sustainable plan for renewable energy within your community using specific textual evidence. Include other energy plans that have contradictory information with your research.

FIGURE 10.3 Pedagogical Flow Map for a Lesson on Communication

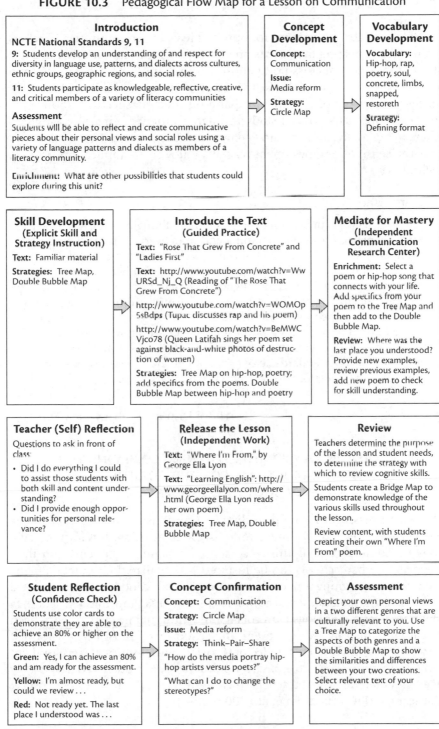

PFMs can also be catalysts for building learning communities. Teachers are now even posting their PFMs on school blogs and on the NUA website, stimulating a sort of cross-pollination within schools, within districts, and among NUA's partner districts. This kind of cross-pollination adds to the teachers' reservoir of resources, expanding their perspectives about how they can approach a unit of study through a variety of engaging activities, intensifying application of the Pedagogy of Confidence. This e-mail conveys the sense of empowerment teachers enjoy from application of these techniques:

March 2010

> After 25 years of teaching and just when I thought that I was all set with my pedagogy style in planning and in delivering Special Education services to students, the way I and many other teaching staff deliver instruction has been revolutionized. Teachers are collaborating more frequently with each other at a higher level than before. There is more meaningful sharing of ideas, artifacts, and planning time among many of us. What seemed like a lesson taught to follow a pacing map has turned into a lesson with a purpose. Pedagogical Flow Maps have helped create a direct connection with the objectives of the lessons and the learning standards across the content areas. Our lessons are more focused; therefore our students are more focused.

> T.W.
> City School District of Albany, New York

CREATING A MEDIATIVE LEARNING COMMUNITY: THE STRUCTURAL CONDUIT FOR THE PEDAGOGY OF CONFIDENCE

The e-mail messages in the preceding section illustrate the efficacy of the Pedagogical Flow Map for mediating discipline learning. But for the Pedagogy of Confidence to flourish—so school-dependent students and their teachers in urban schools can be inspired to actualize their potential—the focus for transforming urban education must go beyond instruction limited to literacy and content acquisition. These students, and the teachers they rely on, are human beings with social and emotional needs that have been consistently disregarded. For them, the school itself must be transformed into an oasis where their intellectual, social, and emotional development can be addressed. This is the oasis school-dependent students so desperately need and their dedicated teachers so earnestly crave (Comer, 1993; Costa & Garmston, 2001; Feuerstein et al., 2006, 2010):

an oasis where the students feel visible, seen, and heard; an oasis that can be a catalyst for tapping the strengths of students and teachers alike; an oasis of trust bonding [teachers, students, and their principal]; an oasis uncontaminated by worry, tension, or stress, where all can actually pay attention—where something other than what is usually expected has the possibility of happening. (Whyte, 2002, CD 4)

In this oasis, affirmation, inspiration, and mediation replace doubt, control, and prescriptive, disengaging remediation. In school, such an oasis takes the form of a Mediative Learning Community.

The word "mediate" is derived from the word "middle." Just like a mediator, a Mediative Learning Community deliberately influences the lives of its school-dependent students and its teachers by providing an environment where the Pedagogy of Confidence can flourish, where strengths are the primary targets of cultivation, and where intellectual growth is optimized (Costa & Garmston, 2007). Schools wherein staff members engage in professional learning communities are primed for transforming practice around more effective methods of instruction through adherence to the "big ideas" that steer their direction. (Some of these big ideas are ensuring that students learn, creating a culture of collaboration, and focusing on results through continuous learning and planning [DuFour & Eaker, 1998].) However, principals of NUA partner schools in urban areas report that they need additional help: They need explicit assistance in research and considerations specifically relevant to their school-dependent students of color, going deeper and spanning more comprehensively to address factors that are barriers to the learning of these individuals. Such factors include poverty, stereotype threats associated with race or ethnicity (Steele & Aronson, 2004), feelings of failure, absence of enrichment, and the stigma associated with the pernicious marginalizing labels applied to their students or associated with their school. These principals seek to establish a community that is acutely aware of the impact of these factors and committed to exploring practices that will mitigate this impact and amplify the innate potential of their students and their teachers. Addressing these needs is the driving force of a Mediative Learning Community.

Addressing the Needs of School-Dependent Students

A Mediative Learning Community is values directed. Research on professional learning communities has shown that one of the best ways for staff members to translate a focus or new direction into practice is through daily in-depth interactions and opportunities that intensify their knowledge and capacity to carry out actions that reflect the new direction (Fullan, 2002). In a Mediative Learning Community, all of the daily practices, structures, and opportunities are designed specifically to bring out the strengths and learning of the students (as manifested through high intellectual performance). At the same time, ongoing efforts enhance staff competence, with the objective of maximizing the staff's ability to support students in developing their motivation for self-directed learning and actualizing their potential. The values of the community are pervasive, and the staff is propelled by a sense of social justice. They are committed to mediating the environment and their own practice to explicitly address the critical considerations that impact the intellectual development, self-directed learning, and self-actualization of their students.

First and foremost, staff members embrace Maslow's (1943) vital tenet that the attributes that generate self-directed learning and self-actualization—such as problem solving, spontaneity, or creativity—cannot develop when students do not feel they are emotionally or physically safe. In a Mediative Learning Community, that concern translates to a dedication on the part of the entire staff to creating emotionally and physically safe environments that will support students' cognitive and social development (Comer, 1993).

Second, a profound belief in the intellectual capacity of the students guides a Mediative Learning Community in addressing the impact of culture on language and cognition.

Third, a Mediative Learning Community generates a new, enabling culture that reflects the cultures of both students and teachers through shared values, rituals, and practices that recognize, esteem, and nurture the capacity of the teachers and the students. This shared culture fosters positive reciprocal relationships that give rise to a purposive system of behaviors that become the norm for the school. Everyone knows what is expected and what is sanctioned, and everyone has a sense of ownership of the standards (Hilliard, 1991/1995; Wilson, 1978).

Fourth, a Mediative Learning Community acknowledges the structural cognitive modifiability, or plasticity, of the brain and focuses its attention on intellectual, cognitive, and emotional development by employing the High Operational Practices of the Pedagogy of Confidence. These seven practices are: (a) identifying and activating student strengths, (b) building relationships, (c) eliciting high intellectual performance, (d) providing enrichment, (e) integrating prerequisites for academic learning, (f) situating learning in the lives of students, and (g) amplifying student voice.

Fifth, a Mediative Learning Community recognizes that self-actualization relies deeply on the social fulfillment that comes from a sense of belonging and esteem. Thus, social development is an explicit objective of the pedagogy applied.

Lastly, a Mediative Learning Community shapes and promotes curricula and opportunities that develop the students' strengths, interests, passions, high intellectual performance, and drive for autonomy.

The Defining Feature of a Mediative Learning Community

A Mediative Learning Community is generated by a shared culture of positive reciprocal relationships. Staff recognize that a true culture of reciprocal relationships can only come about when students are genuine members of the community, and this is the feature that most distinguishes a Mediative Learning Community from a professional learning community. Students are integral members of a Mediative Learning Community—with voice and authentic participation. Staff acknowledge their own personal transformations from the Pedagogy of Confidence. They know that transforming the school into an oasis in which they and their students will thrive requires including students, so they too will develop a sense of investment and responsibility in co-creating a Mediative Learning Community.

Inclusion of students as co-creators of a Mediative Learning Community produces a result similar to what Lave and Wenger (1990) describe as a "community of practice." In both types of communities, staff and students share a passion for what they are collaboratively constructing and facilitating, and they get better at it as they interact regularly. Over time, the collective learning results in teachers and students having shared school practices and developed stronger relations, creating a shared, inclusive culture (Smith, 2003/2009). The difference between a Mediative Learning Community and a community of practice is that teachers and students are distinguished by the role the teachers have in ultimately being responsible for the learning and welfare of their students.

The inclusion of students in a Mediative Learning Community is cultivated through institutionalized opportunities and procedures that empower them to have voice, value, and choice in the directions taken and the decisions made about such things as learning and teaching practices, reshaping curriculum, evaluation, counseling, discipline procedures, and governance. Students' views and their input are initially elicited through surveys, interviews, and focus groups, but these vehicles quickly advance to conduits students have traditionally been excluded from, such as faculty meetings, collaboration with teachers on subcommittees, and, most particularly, participation in professional development and co-teaching. Such engagements are described in Chapter 7 as vehicles for the High Operational Practice of "amplifying student voice."

The commitment of the staff to creation of an intellectually stimulating, collaborative, emotionally secure community for students through authentic engagement fosters an environment for the students that can mitigate the effects of the potentially debilitating challenges they live through outside school. The engagement generates trusting relationships, encouraging teachers and students to fearlessly articulate their perceptions and needs to each other, enabling better understanding of and appreciation for each other's cultural frames of reference, dismantling walls and building bridges between them on which their confidence and self-actualization can thrive.

Cultivating the Environment

The process of establishing Mediative Learning Communities in NUA partner districts began in 2010. Even the most inspirational principals in these districts report that creating a Mediative Learning Community is complex, requiring refinement over time that is directed by strategic, collaborative planning. They recognize that in order to restructure or cultivate the environment to generate a Mediative Learning Community, they must deploy all of their inspirational skills to address the concerns of resistant members of their staff and reculture their awareness, attitudes, beliefs, and perceptions about school-dependent students (Hargreaves, 1994). These leaders begin the reculturation process by conveying to their staff that they do not perceive their schools as having an overabundance of *low*-achieving students but rather a group of *under*achievers who possess plentiful strengths and vast untapped intelligence. The challenge is that these individuals are dependent on the school to help them tap those strengths and expand their intellectual capacity. These leaders also recognize that, like the students, their teachers have emotional needs that must be addressed in a safe, supportive environment where they can develop the competence and confidence to attend to the learning needs of their school-dependent students. These principals demonstrate that they recognize the teachers' needs by enabling professional development that substantiates the three beliefs of the Pedagogy of Confidence: (a) intelligence is modifiable, (b) all students benefit from a focus on high intellectual performance, and (c) learning is influenced by the interaction of culture, language, and cognition.

What is most notable about how these inspirational principals cultivate the environment for acceptance of and inclusion in a Mediative Learning Community is that they courageously let go of the need for control, a need that is so often generated by doubt and fear. These leaders realize that control creates stress and can suppress positive engagement and action. Instead, these leaders use the power of emotions to prevail on the staff to see the benefit of creating a Mediative Learning Community as a vehicle for engaging their adolescent students. They remind the staff that relationships are the very raison d'être for adolescents, and that they are imperative not only for engagement but also for learning, because adolescents are at a crucial stage in the development of the intersection of the social and intellectual components of their brain (Comer, 1993; Feuerstein, 1979a; Sylwester, 2007). They ask their staff to remember and revive their own confidence in their capacity to inspire their students. They remind teachers of the benefits of cultivating a culture of positive reciprocal relationships between themselves and their students. They do all in their power to bring together leaders, teachers, staff, and students so that the school can become that oasis where they all can actualize their full potential.

When teachers act from the Pedagogy of Confidence, they invest in a positive reciprocal relationship with their students by addressing the considerations that impact the students' learning, with an explicit focus on the High Operational Practices for eliciting the strengths, interests, passions, and high intellectual performance that motivate self-directed learning. The students reciprocate through conscious development of their Habits of Mind (Costa & Kallick, 2000)—those dispositions and behaviors that fuel them to engage and follow through for self-directed learning and actualizing their potential.

For the students, this opportunity to authentically co-create a Mediative Learning Community engages them by activating their adolescent psyche— they are granted purpose, choice, ownership, and responsibility (Dweck, 2000; Kanter, 2006; Sylwester, 2007). They begin to feel they are valued and have genuine commerce that they can reinvest in the community.

Priming Students and Staff for Participation

There are numerous implications for the social development of adolescents participating in a Mediative Learning Community, one of the most important being the positive cultural assimilation it facilitates. Being accepted as fully participating members of the community allows students to navigate the cultural complexities of adults by observing adult dispositions and participating in authentic adult social interactions. They learn to master the "real cultural knowledge" of the school by confidently enacting adult behavior through discourse with their teachers. This discourse authorizes them to question adult behaviors, to articulate their desires and perceptions, and to share the frames of reference through which their perceptions developed.

Having students engage in authentic exchange with teachers requires a degree of comfort for both the teachers and the students. This comfort evolves over time through orchestrated engagements. In NUA's San Francisco partnership, engagements were codified through creation of four vehicles to prime students and their teachers for collaborative participation in a Mediative Learning Community, allowing them to ease into the process of fearless exchange. These vehicles were identified as student voice, dialogue, discourse, and guided dialogical thinking.

Student voice. The first priming stage was called simply "student voice" by teachers and students. The NUA mentors knew the process of engaging students would have to evolve organically from interest and trust, so they began by soliciting student perspectives about their learning needs through the mechanics of the student surveys from the NUA Instructional Assessment. The surveys enable the students and their teachers to express their points of view or frames of reference on what personally motivates and affects them within the learning environment, as well as what would help them become more competent and confident in that environment. Written surveys have morphed into video surveys in which students interview each other about their perspectives. The videos have become powerful tools because they allow the students who were the videographers and interviewers to share the perspectives documented in the videos with a broader group of students in various forums, such as student council meetings or student-led assemblies. The videos are also shared with teachers during professional development sessions, providing them access to the actual voices of the students as a complement to the strengths and maturity displayed in the documentation.

Dialogue. The second vehicle for priming student participation is orchestrated dialogue. Dialogue provides the opportunity for students to engage in conversations with their teachers. Teachers are guided to purposefully initiate conversations in which they can discuss specific issues with their students—issues that might have surfaced during the student video interviews, problems whose resolution would benefit from the perspectives of both teachers and students (such as cell phone use in school), or even non-school issues such as community or world events (always potent catalysts for dialogue). Through the dialogue, teachers can become acquainted with student dimensions that traditionally have had limited avenues for expression—dimensions such as their insight, their empathy, their sense of justice, their interests, their motivation to participate in meaningful discussions, and their ability to philosophize, theorize, and hypothesize. These dimensions not only change teachers' perceptions of their students, they also become cultural bridges between the teachers and the students. These new perspectives and bridges stimulate feelings of value and recognition by both the students and the teachers. The relationships motivate teachers to move away from a mind-set of control through punishment to one of understanding through collaboration.

Discourse. The third vehicle for priming is discourse. Discourse differs from dialogue in that students are guided to share their ideas and perspectives through specific protocols and various formats in a variety of group forums with faculty. This discourse facilitates what Colvin (2008) calls "deliberate practice" of language, a process essential for accelerating cognitive and social performance. As language and presentation skills are authentically applied, students appreciate the purpose of these skills, recognizing their currency in enabling them to better articulate their perspectives and ideas so they can be better heard. They are building confidence and competence in the very skills specified as learning targets in various English language arts standards. Additionally, and most importantly, this authentic opportunity for school-dependent students to develop their voice is often the only way of leveling the playing field so they can compete linguistically with their more advantaged peers in the world outside their home community. Many school-dependent students receive no mediated guidance outside of school in clearly and substantively articulating their perspectives, yet this ability is critical if they are to engage successfully in the type of discourse that will give them commerce in the world beyond their peers.

Guided dialogical thinking. The final step in priming students for participation is guided dialogical thinking. This happens through discourse involving students in problem solving, decision making, and teamwork, where they are specifically asked to take a perspective from the teacher's frame of reference to address problems or decisions to be made. Teachers are guided to shift their frame of reference to match that of the students as well. This exchange of ownership of perspectives in a positive, nonjudgmental environment generates new considerations to be analyzed and assessed, expands the realm of possible solutions, and reveals new sets of cause-and-effect relationships that can be explored for decision making. Adolescents develop new perspectives from these interactions with their teachers, and they experience a growing awareness of how they themselves are perceived. These new insights, in turn, affect what Sylwester (2007) regards as the moral and ethical base for the development of their autonomy. For adolescents, these opportunities engage students' executive decision making, which affects the maturation of the frontal lobes of the brain.

NUA mentors assist staff and students in transforming their schools into Mediative Learning Communities through various strategies that scaffold understanding of each of the priming steps. To improve their own effectiveness, the mentors explore ways to optimize presentation of the strategies for co-learning between students and teachers. The most challenging, yet generative, priming step is dialogical thinking. Synectics is a model of teaching that helps students develop facility in the practice of assuming different perspectives and creatively articulating a response to an issue or problem inherent in dialogical thinking. The key feature of synectics is its use of analogies. The idea is to use analogies to develop comfort in making metaphorical comparisons, and then to use analogies to attack problems or issues (Joyce, Weil, & Calhoun, 2009). During one planning session for NUA mentors, classroom management was chosen as the problem to be collaboratively attacked through synectics, in preparation for working teachers and students through experiences in dialogical thinking. One mentor, Camile Earle-Dennis, assumed the perspective of the students, explaining that students personalize problems or issues in school, saying "I . . ." or "we . . . ," whereas teachers depersonalize problems or issues in school, saying "they . . . ." Using dialogical thinking, the mentor synthesized ideas to respond to the issue of classroom management from the perspective of the students, through this poem:

Me Is a Mirrored Reflection of We

Me is on a quest by itself
To save **I** and **my**
From the enemy **we**
Yet,
We stands strong with **they** and **us**
Chanting:
"United **we** stand, divided **we** fall."
"United **we** stand, divided **we** fall."
Although **we** outnumbers **I**
Me and **my** still overcome
Scratching their heads,
We, they and **us**
Stand stupefied
Why?

— Camile Earle-Dennis

THE RECIPROCAL NATURE of a Mediative Learning Community and the relationship it promotes between school-dependent students and their teachers produces many benefits, ranging from creating a shared culture, facilitating mature discourse between students and teachers, and developing collaborative investment in the community. But the benefit to teachers who have committed their lives to working with school-dependent culturally different students—and this is the most compelling, most needed, most transformative catalyst of all—is the benefit of creating bridges between themselves and their students so they can optimize the students' learning potential. Teachers search for ways to make these connections, often with a sense of frustration, often with a sense of desperation, sometimes with a sense of ineptitude. But they do search, asking, "How do we get into the minds of these kids?" Reuven Feuerstein's response is this: "By having 'these kids' get into the minds of the teachers!" In other words, involving students in genuine discourse through engagements that elicit dialogical thinking enables them to see into the frames of reference of the teachers and vice versa—each gaining an appreciation of the other's perspectives, concerns, and insights. This engagement reshapes how students view their environment, their teachers, and their learning and, again, vice versa. The students' responses to these perceptions in turn generate a new lens through which we can view what animates school-dependent adolescents—how we view them, how we see their thinking, how we understand what makes them who they are. From a pedagogical perspective, including students as active members of a Mediative Learning Community enables teachers to use the students' frames of reference to reshape their own thinking, thereby reshaping their practice. In essence, teachers mediate students' learning and students mediate teachers' teaching. This reshaped practice can optimize the inherent intellectual capacities these students possess—opening up rewarding futures for the students and increasing the confidence and satisfaction of the teachers who have worked so hard to help them get there.

11

Waiting to Excel

From Belief, Practices, and Structures to the Pedagogy of Confidence

America was founded on the notion of liberty and equality. We consistently honor the principle of liberty and the world remains inspired. . . . How we educate remains the Gordian knot of America's ability to remain an economic and moral leader in the world. There is the need for a bold strategic stroke if we are to succeed in enabling the promise of America for all of its citizens.

—Eric J. Cooper

What are the possibilities for cultivating the Pedagogy of Confidence in urban education?

I have quoted the words of David Whyte (2002) often throughout this recounting of the odyssey that brought about the Pedagogy of Confidence. The images these words evoke masterfully convey the "what is" of urban education and the "what could be" if we remember what we instinctively know about engaging learning. By confidently applying this knowledge we can inspire all of our students in the same way we inspire our own children to realize their potential.

CONTEXTUALIZING TRANSFORMATION TO REALIZE THE PEDAGOGY OF CONFIDENCE

One of the last citations I present from David Whyte's CD set is a selection aptly entitled "The Key Is Ours: Extraordinary Transformations." In this lecture he uses the metaphor of a swan and the way it maneuvers through its existence to illustrate the transformation process. He eloquently describes how majestic the swan is in the water, but the minute it comes out of the water, moving awkwardly and inelegantly on terra firma, it looks like it does not belong in the world at all (Whyte, 2002, CD 3).

Shortly after first hearing this description of the swan, I visited a lake in England, where what seemed to be hundreds of swans did in fact glide majestically on their journey across the water. Yet, just as Whyte describes, every step they took out of their watery element onto the land, to vie for crumbs from admiring tourists, was conducted with an awkward, inelegant cadence that made them appear as if they were simply incapable of nimbly adapting to the terrain they crossed. As I turned my attention from the waterborne swans that gracefully powered themselves across the surface to the swans following each other haltingly and fretfully out of their element, I thought about how the swans are a keen metaphor for what teachers experience in urban education.

Teachers—who fuel themselves with their belief in the innate intellectual potential of their students and have confidence in their own ability to divine this potential and to propel the students in the direction of learning engagement and growth—are like swans in their element, majestically and artfully gliding through their teaching journey. Unfortunately, however, urban teachers are often compelled out of their element by marginalizing policies, into a landscape littered with practices that ignore the natural learning process and landmines of debilitating controls. When this happens, they are like swans out of water, fretfully stumbling in a seemingly unskillful manner on the unsupportive and hazardous terrain.

Confident teachers, when they find themselves on this unsupportive terrain, move quickly back into their element, risking the landmines they might have to encounter along the way. The moment they are back in their element, they are transformed, assured that the element from which they practice will nourish their resolve and take them to their destination. Other somewhat less confident teachers, when forced onto the unsupportive and unproductive terrain, stumble awkwardly, ineptly, and with great effort—like swans out of water. However, the moment no one is looking, at every chance they get, these teachers re-enter their element and adeptly move toward their destination. Regrettably, these opportunities arise only sporadically, and the longer they are forced to remain out of their element, the more fatigued and stressed they become, losing their footing and their energy. But they wait—wait to once again majestically excel in their element.

Lastly, there are those teachers who have been led to believe that although they are stumbling awkwardly on the rocky and unproductive terrain they are compelled to practice on, their element—the element from which they instinctively seek to practice to enrich and engage learning— is not what their school-dependent students need. They are constantly told that these are "other people's children" (Delpit, 1995), who require restricted instruction that focuses on their weaknesses. So, as graceless as they feel with this blurred and limiting view, they acquiesce, familiarizing themselves with the hazardous, unproductive terrain and adapting to their awkwardness until it becomes their expected way to maneuver.

School-dependent students are like the swans as well. The difference is that millions of them are like swans born out of and never put into the water. They exist denied the element conducive to their learning, the element in which they belong. They spend their school years thinking that the awkward, unskilled existence they experience on the unsupportive terrain of the classroom is just what they were born to—the way it's supposed to be. They never learn to swim because they have been deprived of their element and have had no models. Their teachers practice outside their own element too, never moving in the majestic way they could move within their element. Not only do these swans/students not know how to swim, but a ceiling is placed above them that inhibits them from learning to fly as well. If they ever get the chance to see the water, the element that would be conducive to their learning, they experience a sense of instinctive familiarity. When this happens, many of them wait for the teacher who will glide confidently toward them, inviting them into that element that could support their learning. Sadly, sometimes even with an invitation, many of these students will not enter the element because even though they are instinctively drawn to the water, they have never learned to swim. Out of fear they hold back, because they feel more comfortable ambling awkwardly and unskillfully on the unsupportive terrain, never experiencing the majesty of their potential. Like the teachers who have been out of their element for so long, these students adapt to the learned "futility"—eternally waiting to excel. But if just one teacher persists in extending to these individuals an invitation into the element in which they belong, and if that teacher confidently models the majestic movement that can happen within that element, the students may find themselves building the courage to step in. Or if one teacher nudges other teachers who have been out of their element for what seems an interminable period, these teachers may step back into their element. If these swans out of water can be brought to understand that all they have to do is make that first small leap of faith, then they can experience the extraordinary transformation that is the unfolding of the majestic potential they possess. All they have to do is to take that first step to move into and become part of their element.

The Pedagogy of Confidence is emancipation for us as teachers to operate from within our element—the element we cultivated from our belief in the intellectual capacity of our students and our own ability to divine and mediate this capacity. It is an invitation to students to grow within this element, where all of us belong. It is the fearless expectation that when students enter this element they will manifest their intellectual potential.

The Pedagogy of Confidence creates an ecological perspective or frame of reference from which to view our students and ourselves. It is a perspective from which we can see our students not as data points within a gap, or as low-performing entities, but as intellectual beings waiting to excel and radiate excellence. It is a perspective from which we can see ourselves not as instructors, but as keys to the locks that imprison the excellence within our students—keys that can emancipate that excellence.

The Pedagogy of Confidence is freedom to harvest the strengths within our students and within ourselves. Through artful application of the science of learning we can cultivate High Operational Practices that will elicit the high intellectual performance that motivates our students to self-directed learning and self-actualization.

When an entire staff operates from the Pedagogy of Confidence with school-dependent students, the school becomes a Mediative Learning Community, an oasis where students are affirmed, inspired, and supported—an oasis where:

- Teachers, principals, and students feel they have commerce and their voice is heard
- Teachers feel alive with a sense of remembering and discovering their passion and their ability to inspire
- Teachers and students are uncontaminated by worry, tension, or stress, allowing them to fully embrace experiences so that something other than what is usually expected has the possibility of occurring
- Teachers can balance what is real in the classroom and what they aspire to for themselves and their students
- Students can explore the frontier of their intelligence
- Principals feel confident in using bold language to defend and protect their students and their teachers (Whyte, 2002)

The Pedagogy of Confidence is not a program to be ruminated over to decide if there is a possibility of bringing it to scale. Such ruminations are always truncated by discussions about costs and feasibility of replication that steer attention away from addressing the most critical factor. To stem the tide of underachievement and systematize practice to promote exceptional learning growth, the competence and confidence of the teacher are of paramount importance. If we are to change the learning trajectory of our school-dependent students toward continuous, extraordinary growth, moving beyond merely adequate yearly progress, then we are obliged to invest in helping our teachers to operate from their element. This investment does not happen through imposition of disengaging, unedifying programs. It happens through support and promotion of the competence and confidence of our teachers. Competence and confidence of teachers develop through:

- Reflective professional development anchored in the science of learning that substantiates belief in the innate intellectual capacity of all students
- Reflective feedback that responds to the professional development through application of High Operational Practices to cultivate the innate intellectual capacity of all students
- Establishment of structures that inspire belief and enable the High Operational Practices that develop high intellectual performance and Habits of Mind to motivate self-directed learning and self-actualization in all students

TURNING THE POSSIBILITIES INTO REALITIES

Thirty years ago I was compelled to set out on my odyssey toward the Pedagogy of Confidence. I began by exploring and codifying research (scientific and empirical) that elucidated practices capable of:

- Substantiating the existence and potential of the vast intellectual capacity of underachieving school-dependent students
- Eclipsing the unintentional yet marginalizing side effects of Title I's focus on weaknesses
- Mitigating the effects of the debilitating circumstances that exist outside and within many poverty-stricken urban schools

The world of the 21st century is not the same as that of the 20th century scientifically, culturally, or economically. It is now irrefutable that if America is to extend the global leadership we have enjoyed into the 21st century, we must furnish content and context for learning and teaching that addresses global awareness; creative and innovative skills; financial, economic, and entrepreneurial literacy; and life and career skills (Partnership for 21st Century Skills, 2009). Also discernible is the reality that if we are to sustain our economic and scientific leadership, we no longer have the luxury of investing in such content and context exclusively for the benefit of those students labeled as gifted and talented, especially when that arbitrarily determined percentage of the population is so small (Jackson & Davis, 2009). Our country's advantage could be perpetuated and expanded exponentially through an investment in pedagogy that values and optimizes practices that draw out and strengthen the innate abilities of all students in two areas:

- Creation of new meaning from a variety of media and disciplines, not just construction and communication of meaning from information someone else has accumulated (Eisner, 1994)
- Exercise of the intellectual dispositions that will allow students to act on the meaning they have created so they can specialize, theorize, hypothesize, philosophize, novelize, mobilize, and revolutionize!

In spite of the reality of the benefits of enriching education for all students in the drive to sustain our global leadership, many things in this country have not changed politically or socially. In these spheres, the ideology of the bell curve as justification for sorting the "haves" from the "have nots" has materialized once again through the application of marginalizing language. Now, the label "minority" (a numerical designation) has been replaced in school systems across the country by the condescending term "subgroup" (a term of location designating "under"). The inference drawn from this term remains the same: People branded with this label will never "belong"; they will never be part of "We the people. . . ." This inference is derived not only from the definition of the prefix, but equally from the way the prefix is used in other countries to distinguish people as an "underclass." But this is America, founded on the notion of liberty and equality, so I remain optimistic.

I am optimistic because at this point in history a bold kind of transformation is possible. When 25% of Caucasian high school students drop out, it is indisputable that underachievement is not confined to urban school-dependent students of color, therefore a different kind of attention or view of underachievement just may be on the horizon.

I am optimistic because even the crafters of No Child Left Behind have declared that the translation of the policy into practice has been unsuccessful, requiring extensive overall modification of the law (Hess & Henig, 2008; Rothstein, 2007). So far, the powers in Washington, D.C., have not let go of instituting competition, sanctions, or punitive reprisals that leave students debilitated by the fallout, turning them into de facto losers. Knowing that those actions have not produced the desired outcomes either, politicians have become more vocal in their advocacy for Charter Schools. Support for Charter Schools implies acceptance of the tenets of Charter Schools—tenets such as the need for flexibility of programs, opportunities for prerequisite assistance, and the adoption of a variety of instructional models and options. Thus, I am optimistic that the decision makers will eventually see that these conditions are needed not only for those few Charter Schools and the limited number of students they serve, but for *all* schools so *all* students may benefit.

I am optimistic because the federal government is currently seeking alterations in assessment procedures to reflect the structural modifiability of the brain, "procedures that show not only what students have learned, but also how that achievement has grown over time" (Gewertz, 2010, p. 1), making possible the type of dynamic assessment designed and prescribed by Reuven Feuerstein. I am optimistic because if this type of assessment is authorized, there is a chance that the vast potential of school-dependent students will be recognized, eclipsing the denigrating implications of the term "subgroup."

I am optimistic because many are now ascribing value to the cognitive and neuroscience research that has demonstrated that with the right practices the brain can be rewired and cognitive functions can be modified so the intellectual capacities of all students can be optimized. This realization could result in authorization of mediative programs such as Feuerstein's Instrumental Enrichment to complement more innovative, dynamic assessments.

I am optimistic because the strengths movement—so pervasive in the business world—is now beginning to permeate the minds of educators and policy makers as a possible antidote to the focus on weaknesses.

I am even more optimistic thanks to the courageous superintendents and principals who partner with the National Urban Alliance and who avail themselves of findings such as those of Feuerstein, neuroscientists, and millions of educators over the years who have affirmed the intellectual capacity and resilience of the human brain. These courageous educators are striving to replace the erroneous application of bell curve ideology to education with a J-curve mentality—a commitment to transforming the culture of their system so that all of their students will assume an upward trajectory of development toward high intellectual performance, resulting in there being no "subgroups" (Dweck, 2007; Feuerstein et al., 2010; J.J. Burgard & Associates, n.d.).

But most of all I am optimistic because there are thousands of teachers like Audra Jordan with whom I have worked who majestically demonstrate confidence from within their element. This confidence can draw thousands of other teachers back into that element, where they can be inspired to extraordinary transformation, remembering their gifts, their passion, and their strengths, emboldened to use these gifts to unlock the gifts in their students. I am optimistic because I see thousands of confident teachers joining with their leadership to speak out in bold voices, creating a clarion call heralding belief in the potential of their students, the promise of possibilities that High Intellectual Performance and High Operational Practices (the new "HIP HOP) provide, and the power of self-directed learning and self-actualization for their students and themselves.

One such call has been passionately composed and fearlessly disseminated throughout the San Francisco Unified School District by Assistant Superintendent Francisca Sánchez. She affirms the mission set forth by Superintendent Carlos Garcia in the district's strategic plan, which is transforming the schools of San Francisco. Her poem follows:

at last

our children say the time has come to engage our minds remodel our brains
let our neurons communicate across 21st century terrains and build
new paths to enlightenment

time to reach across place and memory to call open unknown doors
by their hidden name and spark electric life where before
only dark lay claim

the time has come our elders say the time has surely come don't you agree
to emancipate our unlimited potential it's not too late to speak truth to
a world distorted by hate and dying of loneliness in a hall of mirrors
where every pain is contained by the pretense we maintain

still like entangled particles when all is said and done we share an intimate
connection that does not easily permit linear disassociation, our lives are
spiral galaxies weaving together streams of thought with the power to
liberate our unfinished dreams; dreams too often caught in the
fatal curves of an unexamined consciousness

the time has come as carlos said to throw not just a pebble but a rock or
two or fistfuls into the pond of justice why not and set the ripples flowing
inward to lift us up above the plains of amber grain so we can swim
among the endless clouds and like jimi kiss the freedom sky

the time has come to unleash our voices and sing fine as the supremes,
the queen of soul, the king of pop or even the new supreme sister sonia take
your pick whatever makes you MOVE until we rain HIP HOP on amerika
and dare to write our own laws of physics and aspiration can you picture
such a thing can you bring your heart and mind to believe that we own
the ancient alchemy to turn what if into what is

once upon a time not that long ago we did not permit the tyranny of doubt
to chain us to hegemony we knew our destiny and turned hearing into
action when martin said the fierce urgency of now must press us to
seek a future where the many might avoid a cognitive holocaust and
not one child more be lost on the wind-tossed sea of mediocrity

*once upon a time our values were the map we used to guide our paths and
we were fearless in our quest to reach the mountain top even when we
could not see it ourselves we stood side by side with trust and relied on
each other to push us on when by ourselves we might have stopped*

*that once upon a time seems like way back in time and now the time has
come round again to look inside our hearts and find the spark that leads to
a whole new mind that ignites the dark we've been living in the time
has come to unbind our children's minds rewind history and
leave the bell curve forever*

*the hell behind cold gray ashes of a nation's shame laid finally to rest the
cost we've paid has been too stark wouldn't you say a mark pressed like
a trail of tears burning furrows deep in our democracy*

*the time has come to turn the tide of history now in this time this time of
yes we can and yes we did now in this time when his story has become our
story we can recapture our moral strength and inspire those we teach
those we lead feed their passion until it ignites and with brains on fire
achieve higher than anyone could anticipate*

*in this time in our time it's past time to end that tired debate about if
or perhaps or someday and one way or another go directly to
what our students require of us*

*in this time in our time we can rekindle the embers that made us founding
members of a special equation high expectations plus possibility yield
results squared to a higher power*

*in this time in our time we can fashion a new state of matter invent a new
future where we aspire to joy to a better fate that we control that we create
because we ourselves were created for this one purpose to rise above the
mud and mire and motivate our spirits past despair even if we have to
levitate to situate our work in our students' hearts and lives with pride*

*now in this time we can restore confidence and hope denied for centuries
past achieve the incredible if we focus on the miraculous and great that
resides in each of us because we will not be doomed by our dna*

*and last now in this time in our time word to all the haters and 21st century
slave traders who profit off our children's hurt watch your backs we've
re-membered our community and definitively put our brains on blast at last*

*at last the time has come in this time in our time
the time has come at last*

—Francisca Sánchez, August 2009

REMEMBER YOUR PASSION AND YOUR GIFTS. This is our time to use the research, examples, and practices shared in this book to sustain our remembering. In remembering, not only will we experience the "glow" that will revitalize our strength, but its warmth will kindle the Pedagogy of Confidence to keep our promise to our school-dependent students to push them to the "frontier of their intelligence" (Whyte, 2001, CD 1). Let's capitalize on the potency of our collective force to transform educational policy for these students. Remember:

You are the one the students have been waiting for!

References

Alpert, R. D. (1976). *Talking Black*. Rowley, MA: Newbury.

Anderson, E. (2005). Strengths-based educating: A concrete way to bring out the best in students—and yourself. *Educational Horizons, 83*(3), 180–189.

Angier, N. (2009, August 18). Brain is a co-conspirator in a vicious stress loop. *The New York Times*.

Averch, H. A., Carroll, S. J., Donaldson, T. S., Kiesling, H. J., & Pincus, J. (1975). How effective is schooling? A critical synthesis and review of research findings. In D. M. Levine and M. J. Bane (Eds.), *The "inequality" controversy: Schooling and distributive justice* (pp. 63–97). New York: Basic Books.

Bruner, J. (1960/1977). *The process of education*. Cambridge, MA: Harvard University Press:

Buckingham, M., & Clifton, D. (2001). *Now, discover your strengths*. New York: The Free Press.

Burgess, R. (2000). Reuven Feuerstein: Propelling the change, promoting continuity. In A. Kozulin & Y. Rand (Eds.), *Experience of mediated learning: An impact of Feuerstein's theory in education and psychology* (Vol. 6, pp. 147–165). Oxford: Elsevier Science.

Caine, R. N., & Caine, G. (2006). The way we learn. *Educational Leadership, 64*(1), 50–54.

Chopra, D. (2003). *The spontaneous fulfillment of desire*. New York: Harmony Books.

Cobbs, P. M., & Grier, W. H. (1977). *Black rage*. New York: McGraw Hill.

Cohen, G. L., Garcia, J., Apfel, N., & Master, A. (2006). Reducing the racial achievement gap: A social-psychological intervention. *Science, 1*(313).

Collins, J. E. (1961). *The effects of remedial education*. London: University of Birmingham School of Education.

Colvin, G. (2008). *Talent is overrated: What really separates world-class performers from everybody else*. New York: Penguin Group.

Comer, J. (1993). *On the school development program: Making a difference for children*. New York: NCREST, Teachers College, Columbia University. (ERIC Document Reproduction Service No. ED358959.)

Cooper, E. J. (2009). Realities and responsibilities in the education village. In L. C. Tillman (Ed.), *The Sage handbook on African American education* (pp. 435–450). Los Angeles: Sage.

Costa, A. (2009). Prologue. In D. Hyerle, *Visual tools for transforming information into knowledge* (pp. x–xv). Thousand Oaks, CA: Corwin Press.

Costa, A., & Garmston, R. (2001). *Cognitive coaching: A foundation for Renaissance schools*. Norwood, MA: Christopher Gordon.

Costa, A., & Garmston, R. (2007). *Mindful mediation: Conversations that promote self-directedness*. Paper presented at National Urban Alliance Coaches Academy, Alexandria, VA.

Costa, A., & Kallick, B. (2000). *Habits of mind: A developmental series.* Alexandria, VA: Association of Supervision and Curriculum Development.

Delpit, L. (1995). *Other people's children: Cultural conflict in the classroom.* New York: The New Press.

Dewey, J. (1933). *How we think.* New York: D. C. Heath and Co.

Diamond, M. C. (2001). *Response of the brain to enrichment.* Retrieved from http://education .jhu.edu/newhorizons/Neurosciences/articles/Response%20of%20the%20Brain%20 to%20Enrichment/index.html

DuFour, R., & Eaker, R. (1998). *Professional learning communities at work: Best practices for enhancing student achievement.* Bloomington, IN: Solution Tree Press.

Dweck, C. (2000). *Self theories: Their role in motivation, personality, and development.* New York: Psychology Press.

Dyer, W. (2006). *Inspiration: Your ultimate calling.* Carlsbad, CA: Hayes House.

Edmonds, R. (1979). Effective schools for the urban poor. *Educational Leadership, 37*(1), 15–18, 20–24.

Eisner, E. W. (1994). *Cognition and curriculum reconsidered* (2nd ed.). New York: Teachers College Press.

Elementary and Middle Schools Technical Assistance Center. (n.d.). *The disproportionate representation of racial and ethnic minorities in special education.* Retrieved April 2009 from http://www.emstac.org/registered/topic/disproportionality/intro.htm

Feuerstein, R. (1978). *Instrumental enrichment manual.* Baltimore: University Park Press.

Feuerstein, R. (1979a). Cognitive modifiability in retarded adolescents: Effects of instrumental enrichment. *American Journal of Mental Deficiency, 83*(6), 88–96.

Feuerstein, R. (1979b). *The dynamic assessment of retarded performers: The learning potential assessment device, theory, instruments, and techniques.* Baltimore: University Park Press.

Feuerstein, R. (1980). *Instrumental enrichment: An intervention program for cognitive modifiability.* Baltimore: University Park Press.

Feuerstein, R., Falik, L. H., and Feuerstein, R. [S.]. (1998). The learning potential assessment device: An alternative approach to the assessment of learning potential. In R. J. Samuda, R. Feuerstein, A. S. Kaufman, J. E. Lewis, R. J. Sternberg, et al., *Advances in cross-cultural assessment* (pp. 100–161). Thousand Oaks, CA: Sage Publications.

Feuerstein, R., Feuerstein, R. S., & Falik, L. H. (2010). *Beyond smarter: Mediated learning and the brain's capacity for change.* New York: Teachers College Press.

Feuerstein, R., Feuerstein, R. S., Falik, L., & Rand, Y. (2006). *The Feuerstein Instrumental Enrichment Program.* Jerusalem: ICELP Publications.

Feuerstein, R., Rand, R., & Hoffman, M. B. (1980). *The dynamic assessment of retarded performers.* Baltimore, MD: University Park Press.

Field, G. B. (2009). The effects of the use of Renzulli learning on student achievement in reading comprehension, reading fluency, social studies, and science. *International Journal of Emerging Technologies in Learning (iJET), 4*(1), 23–28.

Fisher, B. (1998). *Attention deficit disorder misdiagnosis: Approaching ADD from a brain–behavior/neuropsychological perspective for assessment and treatment.* Boca Raton, FL: CRC Press.

Friere, P. (1970). *Pedagogy of the oppressed.* New York: Herder and Herder.

Fullan, M. (2002). The change leader. *Educational Leadership, 59*(8), 16–20.

Furth, H. G., & Wachs, H. (1974). *Thinking goes to school: Piaget's theory in practice.* Oxford: Oxford University Press.

Gage, F. (2003). Brain, repair yourself. *Scientific American, 289*(3), 46–53.

Gardner, H. (1983/2003). *Frames of mind. The theory of multiple intelligences.* New York: Basic Books.

Gay, G. (2000). *Culturally responsive teaching: Theory, research, & practice.* New York: Teachers College Press.

Gee, J. P. (1991). *Rewriting literacy: Culture and discourse of the other.* New York: Bergin and Garvey.

Gee, J. P. (1996). *Social linguistics and literacies: Ideology in discourses.* Bristol, PA: Taylor and Francis.

Gewertz, C. (2010). Rules urge new style of testing. *Education Week, 29*(29), 1, 17.

Ginsburg, H. (1972). *The myth of the deprived child.* Englewood Cliffs, NJ: Prentice-Hall.

Gladwell, M. (2008). *Outliers.* New York: Little, Brown and Company.

Goldberg, E. (2001). *The executive brain: Frontal lobes and the civilized mind.* New York: Oxford University Press.

Goldstein, K., & Blackman, S. (1978). *Cognitive styles: Five approaches and relevant research.* New York: John Wiley and Sons.

Goleman, D. (1995). *Emotional intelligence: Why it can matter more than I.Q.* New York: Bantam Books.

Hansen, J. W. (1997). Cognitive styles and technology-based education. *Journal of Technology Studies, 23*(1), 14–23. Retrieved from http://scholar.lib.vt.edu/ejournals/JOTS/Winter-Spring-1997/PDF/4-Hansen-article.pdf

Hargreaves, A. (1994). *Changing teachers, changing times: Teachers' work and culture in the postmodern age.* New York: Teachers College Press.

Hattie, J. (2009). *Visible learning: A synthesis of over 800 meta-analyses relating to achievement.* New York: Routledge.

Hess, F., & Henig, J. (2008). 'Scientific research' and policymaking a tool, not a crutch. *Education Week, 27*(22), 26, 36.

Hilliard, A. (1977). Classical failure and success in the assessment of people of color. In M. Coleman (Ed.), *Black children just keep on growing.* Washington, DC: Black Child Development Institute.

Hilliard, A. (1991/1995). The learning potential assessment device and instrumental enrichment as a paradigm shift. In A. Hilliard III (Ed.), *Testing African American students.* Chicago: Third World Press.

Hobbs, N. (1980). Feuerstein's instrumental enrichment; teaching intelligence to adolescents. *Educational Leadership, 37*(7), 566–568.

Hobson v. Hansen, 269 F. Supp. 401 (D.D.C. 1967).

Holloway, M. (2003). The mutable brain. *Scientific American, 289*(3), 79–85.

Hunter, M. (1994). *Enhancing teaching.* New York: Macmillan

Hyerle, D. (2004). *Student successes with thinking maps.* Thousand Oaks, CA: Corwin Press.

Hyerle, D. (2009). *Visual tools for transforming information into knowledge.* Thousand Oaks, CA: Corwin Press.

Jackson, Y. (2001). Reversing underachievement in urban students: Pedagogy of confidence. In A. Costa (Ed.), *Developing minds.* Alexandria, VA: Association for Supervision and Curriculum Development.

Jackson, Y. (2002, December). Comprehension and discipline literacy: The key to high school achievement. *New Horizons for Learning Online Journal, 9*(1). Retrieved from http://www.marthalakecov.org/~building/strategies/literacy/jackson.htm

Jackson, Y., & Davis, A. (2009). *Pedagogy of confidence.* Unpublished manuscript. Syosset, NY: National Urban Alliance.

Jackson, Y., Johnson, T. G., & Askia, A. (2010). Kids teaching kids. *Educational Leadership, 68*(1), 60–63.

Jackson, Y., Lewis, J. E., Feuerstein, R., & Samuda, R. J. (1998). Linking assessment to intervention with instrumental enrichment (pp. 162–196). In R. J. Samuda (Ed.), *Advances in cross cultural assessment.* Thousand Oaks, CA: Sage Publishing.

Jackson, Y., Long, C., & Merrifield, M. (2010). *Collaborative leadership for student success*. Unpublished manuscript. Syosset, NY: National Urban Alliance.

Jackson, Y., & McDermott, V. (2009). Fearless leading. *Educational Leadership, 67*(2), 34–39.

Jensen, E. (1998). *Teaching with the brain in mind*. Alexandria, VA: Association for Supervision and Curriculum Development.

J.J. Burgard & Associates. (n.d.). *The shift to "J curve" mentality*. Retrieved from http://www.jjburgard.com/sub/Support/jcurve2.htm

Johnson, C. (2007, October 19). A clearer picture: Poor eyesight can slow learning. *The Taos News*.

Joyce, B., Weil, M., & Calhoun, E. (2009). *Models of teaching* (8th ed.). Boston: Allyn & Bacon.

Kanter, R. M. (2006). *Confidence*. New York: Three Rivers Press.

Kohn, A. (2008). It's not what we teach, it's what they learn. *Education Week, 28*(3), 26, 32.

Kraschen, S. (1982). Principles and practices in second language acquisition. *Oxford Journals Humanities ELT Journal, 37*(3), 283–285.

Ladson-Billings, G. (1992). Reading between the lines and beyond the pages: A culturally relevant approach to literacy teaching. *Theory into Practice, 31*(4), 312–320.

Ladson-Billings, G. (1994). *The dreamkeepers: Successful teachers of African American children*. San Francisco: Jossey-Bass.

Lafley, A. G., & Charan, R. (2008). *Game changer: How you can drive revenue and profit growth with innovation*. New York: Crown Business.

Lareau, A. (2003). *Unequal childhoods: Class, race, and family life*. Berkeley: University of California Press.

Larry P. v. Riles, 793 F.2d 969 (9th Cir. 1984).

Lave, J., & Wenger, E. (1990). *Situated learning: Legitimate peripheral participation*. Cambridge, UK: Cambridge University Press.

Learning First Alliance. (2001). *Every child learning: Safe and supportive schools*. Retrieved April 2009 from http://www.learningfirst.org

Levine, D. M., & Bane, M. J. (Eds.). (1975). *The "inequality" controversy: Schooling and distributive justice*. New York: Basic Books.

Lidsky, T. I., & Schneider, J. S. (2005). Adverse effects of childhood lead poisoning: The clinical neuropsychological perspective. Retrieved July 2009 from http://www.sciencedirect.com

Link, F. (1981). *The awareness workshop on instrumental enrichment*. Presented at Association of Supervision and Curriculum Development National Convention, St. Louis, MO.

Mahiri, J. (1998). *Shooting for excellence*. New York: Teachers College Press.

Mahiri, J. (Ed.). (2004). *What they don't learn in school: Literacy in the lives of urban youth*. New York: Peter Lang.

Mahiri, J. (2006). Digital DJ-ing: Rhythms of learning in an urban school. *Language Arts, 84*(1), 55–62.

Marzano, R. (2004). *Building background knowledge*. Alexandria, VA: Association for Supervision and Curriculum Development.

Maslow, A. H. (1943). A theory of human motivation. *Psychological Review, 50*(4), 370–396.

Maxwell, L. (2010). Turnaround funds flowing to state coffers. *Education Week, 29*(29), 1, 28.

McIntyre, T. (1996). Does the way we teach create behavior disorders in culturally different students? *Education and Treatment of Children, 19*(3), 354–370. Retrieved from http://www.behavioradvisor.com/C-Learn.html

Medina, J. (2008). *Brain rules: 12 principles for surviving and thriving at work, home, and school*. Seattle: Pear Press.

Meyers, E. (1966). Self-concept, family structure and school achievement: A study of disadvantaged Negro boys (Doctoral dissertation, Columbia University). *Dissertation
Abstracts International, 27*, 11A, 3960. (University Microfilms No. 67-5540.)

Narrol, H. G., & Giblon, S. T. (1984/2001). *The fourth "R": Uncovering hidden learning
potential*. Baltimore: University Park Press.

National Board for Professional Teaching Standards (NBPTS). 2003. *Adolescence and young
adulthood English language arts standards* (2nd ed.). Arlington, VA: National Board for
Professional Teaching Standards. Retrieved from http://www.nbpts.org/userfiles/File/
aya_ela_standards.pdf

National Center for Fair & Open Testing (FairTest). (2008). *Independent test results show
NCLB failing*. Boston: Author.

National Institute of Child Health and Human Development (NICHD) & National Council for the Accreditation of Teacher Education (NCATE). (2006). *Child and adolescent
development research and teacher education: Evidence-based pedagogy, policy, and practice*.
Washington, DC: Author.

National Urban Alliance. (2001). *Briefing book*. Unpublished manuscript. Syosset, NY:
Author.

National Urban Alliance. (2010). *Proposal to the Kellogg Foundation*. Unpublished reference
paper. Syosset, NY: Author.

Nieto, S. (2009). From surviving to thriving: How teachers learn. *Educational Leadership,
66*(5), 8–13.

No Child Left Behind Act of 2001 [NCLB]. 20 U.S.C. §6301 et seq.

Noguera, P. (2003). *City schools and the American dream*. New York: Teachers College Press.

Noguera, P. (2008, March). *Creating conditions that promote student achievement*. Speech
presented at the Teaching for Intelligence Conference, Albany, NY.

North Central Regional Educational Laboratory (NCREL). (1996). *Critical issue: Providing
effective schooling for students at risk*. Retrieved from http://www.ncrel.org/sdrs/areas/
issues/students/atrisk/at600.htm.

Orem, R. C. (1967). *Montessori for the disadvantaged*. New York: Capricorn Books.

Orfield, G., Losen, D., Wald, J., & Swanson, C. B. (2004). *Losing our future: How minority
youth are being left behind by the graduation rate crisis*. Cambridge, MA: Civil Rights
Project at Harvard University.

Palmer, E., & Zoffer, G. (2004). *WMEP adult learning: National Urban Alliance 2003–2004.
Evaluation report*. Edina, MN: Aspen Associates.

Partnership for 21st Century Skills. (2009). *Framework for 21st century learning*. Retrieved
February 2009 from http://www.p21.org/index.php?option=com_content&task=view
&id=254&Itemid=119

Patterson, K., Grenny, J., Maxfield, D., McMillan, R., & Switzler, A. (2008). *Influencer: The
power to change anything*. New York: McGraw-Hill.

Peart, K. N. (2006). Racial achievement gap dramatically altered with affirmation exercise.
Science, 313(5791).

Piaget, J. (1950). *The psychology of intelligence*. New York: Routledge.

Pink, D. H. (2005). *A whole new mind: Why the right-brainers will rule the future*. New York:
Riverhead Books.

Pogrow, S. (2000). Beyond the *'good* smart' mentality: Overcoming the cognitive wall.
Education Week, 19(32), 44, 46–47.

Reisner, E. (1980). *The Office of Education administers change in law: Agency response to Title
I, ESEA amendments of 1978*. Washington, DC: The National Advisory Council on the
Education of Disadvantaged Children.

Renzulli, J. S. (n.d.). *The three-ring conception of giftedness: A developmental model for creative productivity.* Retrieved August 2009 from http://www.gifted.uconn.edu/sem/pdf/The _Three-Ring_Conception_of_Giftedness.pdf

Renzulli, J. S. (1975). Talent potential in minority group students. In W. Barbe & J. Renzulli (Eds.), *Psychology and education of the gifted.* New York: Irvington.

Renzulli, J. S. (1978). What makes giftedness? Reexamining a definition. *Phi Delta Kappan, 60*(3), 180–184, 261.

Renzulli, J. S. (1982). What makes a problem real: Stalking the illusive meaning of qualitative differences in gifted education. *Gifted Child Quarterly, 26*(4), 148–156.

Renzulli, J. S. (1983). Guiding the gifted in the pursuit of real problems: The transformed role of the teacher. *The Journal of Creative Behavior, 17*(1), 49–59.

Renzulli, J. S. (1994). *Schools for talent development: A practical plan for total school improvement.* Mansfield Center, CT: Creative Learning Press.

Renzulli, J. S., & Reis, S. M. (2007). A technology based program that matches enrichment resources with student strengths. *iJET International Journal of Emerging Technologies in Learning, 3*(2).

Richhart, Ron. (2002). *Intellectual character.* San Francisco, CA: Jossey-Bass.

Rodriquez, E. R., & Bellanca, J. (1996). *What is it about me you can't teach?* Palatine, IL: IRI/SkyLight Training and Publishing.

Rothstein, R. (2007). Leaving "No Child Left Behind" behind. *The American Prospect.* Retrieved August 2009 from http://www.prospect.org/cs/articles?article=leaving_nclb _behind

Samuda, R. J. (1998). Cross-cultural assessment: Issues and alternatives. In R. J. Samuda (Ed.), *Advances in cross-cultural assessment* (pp. 1–19). Thousand Oaks, CA: Sage Publishing.

San Francisco Unified School District (SFUSD). (2008). *Beyond the talk: Taking action to educate every child now. SFUSD 2008–2012 strategic plan.* San Francisco: San Francisco Unified School District. Retrieved from http://portal.sfusd.edu/template/default.cfm ?page=home.strategic_plan

San Francisco Unified School District (SFUSD). (2009). *San Francisco Unified School District LEA Plan. Moving beyond the talk to RESULTS: Reaching Educational Success and Unlimited Leadership: Targeting Sustainability.* San Francisco: San Francisco Unified School District. Retrieved from http://www.beyondthetalk.org/institute/learning-strands/ learning-strands/082609_leaplan_copy.pdf

Sapolsky, R. (2003). Taming stress. *Scientific American, 289*(3), 87–95.

Schütz, R. (2007). *Stephen Kras[c]hen's theory of second language acquisition.* Retrieved August 2009 from http://www.sk.com.br/sk-krash.html

ScienceDaily. (2009, January 27). Early childhood stress has lingering effects on health. Retrieved August 20, 2009, from http://www.sciencedaily.com/releases/2009/01/ 090126173606.htm

SIL International. (1999). *Schema theory of learning.* Retrieved from http://www.sil.org/ lingualinks/literacy/ImplementALiteracyProgram/SchemaTheoryOfLearning.htm

Skinner, B. F. (1974). *About behaviorism.* New York: Random House.

Slade v. Board of Education of Hartford County, 252 F.2d 291 (4th Cir. 1958).

Smith, C. (1999). *Assessing and reporting progress through student-led portfolio conferences. National Middle School Association (NMSA).* Retrieved from http://www.nmsa.org/ Publications/WebExclusive/Portfolio/tabid/650/Default.aspx

Smith, E., & Crozier, K. (1998). Ebonics is not Black English. *Western Journal of Black Studies, 22*(2), 109–116.

Smith, M. K. (2003/2009). Communities of practice. *The encyclopedia of informal education*. Retrieved from http://www.infed.org/biblio/communities_of_practice.htm.

Smith, S. (2010). *Violence weighs heavy on a child's mind*. Retrieved from http://paging drgupta.blogs.cnn.com/2010/06/14/embargoed-monday-614-3pm-violence-weighs -heavy-on-a-childs-mind/

Steele, C., & Aronson, J. (2004). *The stereotype threat*. Retrieved from http://www.mtholyoke .edu/offices/comm/csj/092404/steele.shtml

Stengel, R. (2008). *Mandela: His 8 lessons of leadership*. Retrieved September 2009 from http://www.Time.com/time/world/article/0,8599,1821467,00.html

Sternberg, R. (1998). All intelligence testing is "cross-cultural": Constructing intelligence tests to meet the demands of person × task × situation interactions. In R. Samuda (Ed.), *Advances in cross-cultural assessment* (pp. 197–217). Thousand Oaks, CA: Sage Publications.

Sternberg, R. J. (2006). Recognizing neglected strengths. *Educational Leadership, 64*(1), 30–35.

Subconscious Secrets. (2004). *Affirmation: Beginners' tool to reprogram the subconscious mind*. Retrieved October 2009 from http://www.subconscious-secrets.com/affirmation.php

Sylwester, R. (2007). *The adolescent brain: Reaching for autonomy*. Thousand Oaks, CA: Corwin Press.

Taylor, O., & Latham-Lee, D. (1991). Standardized tests and African-American children: Communication and language issues. In A. G. Hilliard III (Ed.). *Testing African-American students*. Chicago: Third World Press.

Teacher's Mind Resources. (n.d.). *The meaning of education*. Retrieved September 2009 from http://www.teachersmind.com/Education.html

Toppo, G. (2008, December 8). Poverty dramatically affects children's brains. *USA Today.*

Torrance, E. P. (1977). *Creativity in the classroom*. Washington, DC: National Education Association.

Vygotsky, L. S. (1978). *Mind in society*. Cambridge, MA: Harvard University Press.

Weiner, B. (1984). An attribution theory of achievement, motivation, and emotion. *Psychological Review, 92*, 548–573.

Weiner, B. (1990). Attribution theory in personality psychology. In L. Perrin (Ed.), *Handbook of personality: Theory and research* (pp. 465–485). New York: Guilford Press.

West Metropolitan Education Program (WMEP). (1989). *About WMEP*. Retrieved May 2009 from http://www.wmep.k12.mn.us/wmepabout.html

Wheeler, R., & Swords, R. (2006). *Code switching: Teaching standard English in urban classrooms*. Urbana, IL: National Council of Teachers of English.

Whyte, D. (2002). *Clear mind, wild heart: Finding courage and clarity through poetry* [CDs]. Boulder, CO: Sounds True.

Wilson, A. N. (1978). *The developmental psychology of the black child*. New York: Africana Research Publications.

Wolf, M. (2007). *Proust and the squid*. New York: Harper Perennial.

Wolfe, P. (2001). *Brain matters: Translating research into classroom practice*. Alexandria, VA: Association for Supervision and Curriculum Development.

Yatvin, J. (2003). I told you so: The misinterpretation and misuse of the National Reading Panel report. *Education Week, 22*(33), 44–45, 56.

Index

About the Author

YVETTE JACKSON is internationally recognized for her work in assessing and actualizing the learning potential of disenfranchised urban students. Changing this reality for these students to one in which their intellectual potential is believed in, valued, and optimized has been Dr. Jackson's calling for her entire career. She has applied her research in neuroscience, gifted education, literacy, and the cognitive mediation theory of Dr. Reuven Feuerstein to develop integrated processes that engage and elicit high intellectual performance from underachievers. She designed the New York City Board of Education's Gifted Programs Framework when she served as Director of Gifted Programs. As New York City's Executive Director of Instruction and Professional Development, she led the creation and implementation of the Comprehensive Education Plan, which maximized the delivery of all core curriculum and support services in the Public Schools of New York City.

Dr. Jackson currently serves as the Chief Executive Officer of the National Urban Alliance for Effective Education, founded at the College Board and Teachers College, Columbia University. She works with school district superintendents, administrators, teachers, and students across the country to customize and deliver systemic approaches that enable students to demonstrate high intellectual performance. She created the Pedagogy of Confidence, whose principles and practices enable educators to accelerate the intellectual development and academic achievement of the students they serve.

Dr. Jackson has been a visiting lecturer at Harvard University's Graduate School of Education, and she served as a member of ASCD's Differentiated Instruction Cadre. She is a keynote presenter at national and international conferences. She has been published in numerous educational journals.

Dr. Jackson received a B.A. from Queens College of the City University of New York with a double major in Education and French. She was awarded a M.A. in Curriculum, an Ed.M. in Educational Administration, and a Doctorate in Educational Administration from Teachers College, Columbia University.